FIRST AID IN SPELLING

**Jan Gallow &
Karen Morrison**

HODDER
EDUCATION
AN HACHETTE UK COMPANY

Every effort has been made to trace all copyright holders, but if any have been inadvertently overlooked the Publishers will be pleased to make the necessary arrangements at the first opportunity.

Orders: please contact Bookpoint Ltd, 130 Milton Park, Abingdon, Oxon OX14 4SB. Telephone: (44) 01235 827720. Fax: (44) 01235 400454. Lines are open 9.00–5.00, Monday to Saturday, with a 24-hour message answering service. Visit our website at www.hoddereducation.co.uk.

First published in 2012 by
Hodder Education,
An Hachette UK Company
338 Euston Road
London NW1 3BH

Impression number   5 4 3
Year   2016 2015 2014 2013

Illustrations by Phoenix Photosetting
Typeset in 11/14 pt ITC Garamond Book by Phoenix Photosetting, Chatham, Kent ME4 4TZ
Printed and bound by CPI Group (UK) Ltd, Croydon, CR0 4YY

A catalogue record for this title is available from the British Library.

ISBN: 978 1444 16893 8

Contents

Contents

English spelling

1. Why is correct spelling important?

Correct spelling is important because it allows you to communicate your thoughts and ideas clearly in writing. Incorrect spelling makes your writing difficult to read and understand.

When people try to read something with lots of misspelt words, they get a bad impression. The content, message and even good ideas in the writing are ignored because the poor spelling makes the reader think that you have nothing important to say.

In school, good spelling is important because it helps you to get better grades. When you take the time to check your work and make sure most words are spelt correctly you give a good impression and you are more likely to get higher marks for written work.

Some people think spelling is not important because they use computers and the computer has a spell checker to find their mistakes. But, the reality is that even with computers you need to be able to spell and spot mistakes in your writing. A computerised spell checker does not check for meaning, only for spelling. Read this sentence to see how a spell checker can let you down: *The spell chequer on my pea sea finds awl the mist aches eye kin not sea.*

Exercise 1			

Do this quick exercise to see how well you spell.

Find the correctly spelt word in each group.

1. sure	shure	shoer	shuer
2. loseing	losing	lozing	loossing
3. hite	height	hight	heighth
4. therefor	there-fore	therefore	therfore
5. forine	foriegn	foreign	forieng
6. beleave	beleve	believe	beleive

2. How to learn spelling

English spelling can be quite difficult to learn because English has adopted sounds and words from many different languages. This makes it difficult to have a set of simple rules for spelling in English. For every rule you learn there will be some words that don't follow the rule.

The good news is that anyone can learn to spell with some patience and practice. You can be a good speller if you find a method of learning to spell that works for you. Try each of the methods in this section to find the method (or methods) that works best for you.

Before you start

Remember:

◆ The letters a, e, i, o and u are vowels.

◆ All the other letters of the alphabet are consonants.

◆ The letter y acts like a vowel *or* a consonant depending on its sound and its position in the word. When y is at the beginning of a word it acts like a consonant and sounds like 'yuh'. For example: yard, yawn, yes, yellow. When the y is in the middle or at the end of a word and it sounds like e or i it acts like a vowel. For example: baby, chatty, day, try.

Method A: Pronounce the sounds

You can remember how to spell some words by saying the word aloud. Speak clearly. Over-exaggerate the pronunciation of each sound. There are some tricky words where certain sounds are not heard. It helps to stress these sounds and make up your own way of pronouncing the word.

The underlined consonants in these words are often not heard:

government   recognise   Wednesday

The underlined vowels in these words are often left out:

noticeable   privilege   separate

Can you hear the double consonants in these words?

better   floppy   mammal   rabbit

Word list			
called	exceed	judgement	really
boundary	granddad	jumped	school
definitely	humorous	narrator	stopped
different	immediate	noticeable	suddenly
embarrass	interesting	people	when

Exercise 2

a. Write the words from the list on page 2 and circle the sounds that are difficult to hear in each word.

b. Read the words again. This time over-exaggerate the pronunciation of each sound.

Method B: Break words into smaller parts (syllabification)

Breaking words into smaller parts (syllables) can help you spell them correctly. Say each syllable clearly and slowly or clap out the syllables in the words.

gov • ern • ment   rec • og • nise   un • der • stand

Each syllable usually has one vowel sound:

no • tice • able   priv • i • lege   sep • a • rate

Double consonants are usually split:

bet • ter   flop • py   mam • mal   rab • bit

Word list

accommodate	children	going	possession
animal	environment	little	practical
another	explanation	looking	something
began	garden	occasion	window
business	giant	opportunity	written

Exercise 3

a. Clap out the syllables of each word in the list above.

b. Write the words and divide them into syllables.

c. Say the words slowly and over-exaggerate the sound of each syllable.

Method C: Use your senses

Use as many of your senses as possible to help you remember how to spell words.

See the word. **Say** the word. **Hear** the word. **Touch** the word.

Follow these steps to learn how to spell words using your senses.

Draw a table like this:

Copy	Say	Test	Correct

Then:

◆ Say the word.

◆ Copy the word into the Copy column.

◆ Say the word using rhythm. Place a ✔ in the Say column if you can say the word. Place an ✗ in the column if you cannot say the word. Ask someone to teach you how to pronounce it correctly.

◆ Use your finger to trace over the word in the Copy column.

◆ Cover the word and write it in the Test column.

◆ Mark the word. Tick it if you spelt it correctly. Write it correctly in the Correct column if you spelt it incorrectly.

◆ Add difficult words to the table a number of times.

◆ As your confidence grows, try doing two or three words at the same time.

After learning three words your table may look like this:

Copy	Say	Test	Correct
friend	✔	freind ✗	friend
occasion	✔	occasion ✔	
success	✔	success ✔	

Try adapting this method to include the pronunciation and syllabification methods.

Draw a table like this:

Copy	Break up	Test	Correct

Then:

◆ Say the word.

◆ Copy the word into the Copy column.

◆ Say the word using rhythm.

◆ Use your finger to trace over the word in the Copy column.

◆ Break up the word into syllables and write it in the Break up column. Say the word, exaggerating the pronunciation.

◆ Cover the word and write it in the Test column.

◆ Mark the word. Tick it if you spelt it correctly. Write it correctly in the Correct column if you spelt it incorrectly.

After learning three words your table may look like this:

Copy	Break up	Test	Correct
soccer	soc • cer	soccer ✔	
image	im • age	image ✔	
explanation	ex • pla • na • tion	explanasion ✗	explanation

Exercise 4

a. Use the 'Copy – Say – Test – Correct' method to learn how to spell these words:

tough, laughed, cough, enough, taught

b. Use the 'Copy – Break up – Test – Correct' method to learn how to spell these words:

across, surprise, address, exercise, exaggerate

Method D: Use memory tricks (mnemonics)

Creating a rhyme or phrase can help you remember how to spell difficult or confusing words. The sillier rhymes are often the easiest to remember.

Word list

address	effect	hear	rhythm
affect	eight	here	separate
believe	February	height	stationary
cemetery	friend	necessary	stationery
desert	gauge	piece	their
dessert	grateful	rhyme	there

Exercise 5

a. Match words from the list on page 5 to each memory trick.

cemetery – I have three 'e's because a lady walked past the cemetery and
screamed *e-e-e*!

_____ – There is a **lie** in me.

_____ – People smell **a rat** in me.

_____ – I am **s**andy with one **s**.

_____ – Another name for me is **sweets** with two 's's.

_____ – I have a fatty and a thinny and a **ght.**

_____ – I am a part of the **pie**.

_____ – **a** and **u** stay in alphabetical order when you spell me.

b. Use words from the list to help you complete these memory tricks.

Keep great out of _____.

Really **h**ope ye _____s with **me**.

R_____ has your **two** **hips** **m**oving.

Always **add** me to your _____.

A _____ is with you until the **end**.

c. Which confusing words do these clues help you spell?

I hear with my **ear**, but there is no ear over **here**.

Pens and pencils are station**e**ry, but a **car** can stand station**a**ry.

The n**oo**se around your neck better be l**oo**se. I lose **one** sock.

**d. Think of memory tricks that you can use to remember how to spell these
words:**

ne**cess**ary, Feb**r**uary, th**ei**r, there

Method E: Picture the word (visualise)

Picturing words can help you remember how to spell them.

◆ Identify the tricky parts of the word.

◆ Write the word and make the tricky parts stand out in some way.

 hum⊙r⊙us   po𝕊𝕊e𝕊𝕊ion   sep𝔸rate

Then:

◆ Say the word. Emphasise the tricky parts in some way.

◆ Close your eyes and picture the word with its tricky parts.

◆ Spell the word aloud emphasising the tricky parts.

◆ Turn over the page and write the word.

◆ Mark the word.

◆ Repeat the process if you spelt the word incorrectly.

Exercise 6

Picture these words to help you remember how to spell them:

   height, definite, desperate, bicycle

a. Say the words and identify the tricky parts.

b. Write the words and make the tricky parts stand out.

c. Follow the rest of the steps in the process.

d. Does picturing the word help you to spell correctly?

Method F: Play with the letters

Playing with the letters in words can help you learn how to spell them. Try this method:

◆ Say the word.

◆ Write the word, saying each letter. d e c o d e

◆ Leave a line.

◆ Say the word.

◆ Say each letter. Write each letter except for the last one. Draw a line in place of the letter. d e c o d _

◆ Leave a line.

◆ Say the word.

◆ Say each letter including the missing letter. Write each letter except for the last two letters. Draw a line in place of the two missing letters. d e c o _ _

◆ Continue in this way until you have no letters, only lines. _ _ _ _ _ _

◆ Now start at the top of your page. Say and spell the word.

◆ Fold over the top of the page so you cannot see the whole word.

◆ Say and spell the word. Fill in the missing letter.

◆ Fold over the page again.

◆ Say and spell the word. Fill in the two missing letters.

◆ Continue in this way until you have written the whole word.

◆ Check that you have spelt it correctly.

Exercise 7

a. **Part of the process has been done for you. Copy and complete the rest of the process. Cover the completed steps before you complete the next step.**

f l i g h t

f l i g h _

f l i g _ _

f l i _ _ _

f l _ _ _ _

f _ _ _ _ _

_ _ _ _ _ _

b. **Now, try using the whole process to learn how to spell these words:**
foreign, difficult, argument

Method G: Find words within words

Finding words within words can help you remember how to spell words correctly.

Word list

ambition	fortunate	paper	transportation
bear	great	pronunciation	water
began	illegal	psychic	want
courage	instead	restaurant	when
dangerous	kilogram	shouted	where
delivery	language	student	white
dragon	metaphor	things	year

Exercise 8

a. **Write the words in the word list and say them.**

b. **Find words within each word and underline them.**

   For example: w<u>ate</u>r.

c. **Write memory tricks to help you remember how to spell three of the words.**

   For example: She ate **water** for breakfast! What sort of breakfast is that?

Method H: Imprint the correct spelling

Marking incorrect spelling and then reinforcing the correct spelling can help you remember tricky spellings that you often get wrong.

Follow these steps to use this method.

◆ Write the incorrectly spelt word five times with the spelling mistake in capital letters.

◆ Put a cross through the spelling mistake.

◆ Next write the word five times with the mistake corrected. Use capital letters for the correction.

◆ Circle the correction.

The example on page 10 shows you how this can be used to learn to spell the word 'desperate'.

Step 1:

DespArate   DespArate   DespArate   DespArate   DespArate

Step 2:

Desp✗rate   Desp✗rate   Desp✗rate   Desp✗rate   Desp✗rate

Step 3:

DespErate   DespErate   DespErate   DespErate   DespErate

Step 4:

Desp(E)rate   Desp(E)rate   Desp(E)rate   Desp(E)rate   Desp(E)rate

This method works because crossing out the wrong letter tells your brain that it doesn't belong. Circling the correct letter trains your brain to remember the correct spelling.

Exercise 9

Use the 'imprinting the correct spelling' method to learn how to spell these words. The incorrect spelling is given first and the correct spelling is given second.

calendEr	calendAr
bYcycle	bIcycle
paraLeLL	paraLLeL
restUArant	restAUrant
sepErate	sepArate

3. Using a dictionary

A dictionary can help you to improve your spelling. To use your dictionary properly you need to know how it works. You also need to know what to do to find words when you are not sure how to spell them.

We recommend the *Chambers Primary Dictionary* (Chambers Harrap Publishers Ltd, 2008) because it is simple and easy to use, but you can use any good dictionary to improve your spelling and vocabulary.

How a dictionary works

The words in a dictionary are listed in alphabetical order. There is normally a guide or key word at the top of each page. These show you the first and/or last word on the page so you can see whether the word you are looking for will be on that page.

Look at this entry from the *Chambers Primary Dictionary* and read the information to find out what the different parts of the entry tell you.

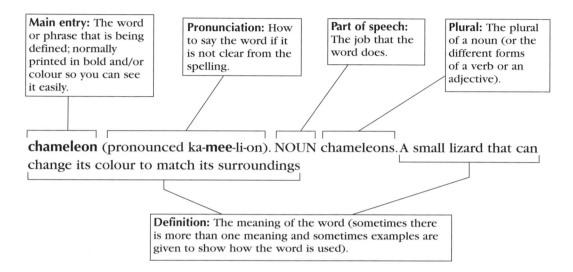

Main entry: The word or phrase that is being defined; normally printed in bold and/or colour so you can see it easily.

Pronunciation: How to say the word if it is not clear from the spelling.

Part of speech: The job that the word does.

Plural: The plural of a noun (or the different forms of a verb or an adjective).

chameleon (pronounced ka-**mee**-li-on). NOUN chameleons. A small lizard that can change its colour to match its surroundings

Definition: The meaning of the word (sometimes there is more than one meaning and sometimes examples are given to show how the word is used).

Finding a word in the dictionary

Imagine you are listening to the radio and you hear a word that sounds like this: i-normus. You want to know how to spell it. How can you use your dictionary to help you?

Follow these steps to find words that you don't know how to spell:

◆ Pronounce the word aloud syllable by syllable – ih-nor-mous. This allows you to work out what the vowel sounds are in each syllable.

◆ Write down how you think the word is spelt. I-normus could be spelt like this:
   inormus   inormous   enormos   enormus

◆ Look in the dictionary. You won't find the word under i because it starts with an e. Even though none of the guesses above are correct, you will find the correct spelling if you look for words starting with enor-. Your dictionary will give you the correct spelling: enormous.

If you have your own dictionary you can make a small pencil mark next to each word when you look it up. Next time you look, you can see whether or not you've had to look up this word before. If you find that you have to keep looking up the same word in your dictionary, add it to your personal spelling dictionary (see page 12) and learn to spell it.

Do *not* mark words in a dictionary that does not belong to you – if you are using a dictionary belonging to your school, a library or another person you should never write in it.

Making a personal spelling dictionary

It is very useful to make your own personal spelling dictionary.

◆ Find a suitable notebook.

◆ Write one letter of the alphabet at the top of each page. (Depending on the size of the notebook, you may have more pages for letters that are used more frequently.)

◆ Write the correct spelling of any words that you misspell or struggle with under the correct letters.

◆ Learn to spell these words.

◆ Use your personal spelling dictionary to quickly find and check spellings if you are unsure.

Exercise 10

a. Make a list of words that you often misspell.

b. Find each word in a dictionary. Follow the steps on page 11 to help you.

c. Write the correct spelling of each word in the correct place in your personal spelling dictionary.

d. Use the method you find most useful to learn the spelling of the words that you have found.

Phonetic rules

There are 26 letters in the alphabet: 5 vowels and 21 consonants. The way letters are combined makes the 44 different sounds we use in English. The sounds have similar spelling patterns, so when you know the sounds made by different letter combinations, you can easily work out how to spell the words. In this chapter you will learn about sounds and see which letters are used to make each sound. This will help you pronounce and spell words correctly.

1. Vowel sounds

Almost half of the sounds in English are vowel sounds. The five vowels: a, e, i, o and u can be used alone, or combined with other vowels or consonants to make different sounds. Knowing how the sounds work and how letters are combined to make these sounds can help you to spell better.

Short vowel sounds

When a vowel appears on its own at the start of a word or in a word or a syllable it normally has a short sound. The short vowels sound like this:

ah eh ih oh uh

For example:

apple   b**e**d   **i**nk   d**o**g   b**u**n

Words with short vowel sounds are normally easy to sound out and spell.

Word list			
apple	van	pin	bun
bat	egg	thin	bug
can	bell	win	much
hat	elephant	pot	mum
lap	except	not	plum
mat	ink	log	tub
pan	pill	orange	umbrella

Exercise 1

a. Write down three words from the list above that have a:

short a sound, short e sound, short i sound, short o sound, short u sound

b. Add three words of your own to each set of examples.

Long vowel sounds

Vowels also have long sounds. A long vowel generally sounds like the way you say the letters when you recite the alphabet. For example:

ay ee eye owe you

There are three main ways of making long vowel sounds:

◆ the silent e

◆ the letter y

◆ double vowels.

The silent e: In most words, a silent e at the end of the word gives a single vowel that appears before it a long sound. You can hear how this works if you read the following words out loud. The words on the left in each pair are words with short vowel sounds from the word list on page 13.

bat	bate		pin	pine
can	cane		thin	thine
hat	hate		win	wine
mat	mate		not	note
pan	pane		plum	plume
van	vane		tub	tube

The letter y: The letter y can act like a consonant or a vowel. In words like yoyo and yacht it acts like a consonant. In words like cry and bye it acts like a vowel.

◆ The silent e also makes the letter y sound like a long i sound.

bye   lyre   type   style

◆ When the y is at the end of a word with two or more syllables, it sounds like a long i if the syllable with the y is stressed.

comply   defy   multiply   supply

◆ If the syllable with the y is not stressed, the y sounds more like a long e.

funny   happy   lolly   mummy   tidy

Exercise 2

The words below have both short and long vowel sounds. Write the words and circle the ones with short vowel sounds. Underline the words with long vowel sounds. Note that some words have both.

ape	funny	odd	these
bake	got	pen	type
cap	hope	pin	tyre
cape	hop	pine	use
cake	ice	price	up
complete	lane	run	vine
dam	let	rent	wet
dame	mat	rice	white
end	melt	rise	winter
every	mite	site	yes
fire	nun	sit	zebra
fore	nose	spy	
for	ore	tale	

Double vowels: Long vowel sounds can also be made by putting two (or more) vowels (including y) together to make a new sound. For example:

air   ear   pool   chief   tree   day   boat   hour   mouse   play

When two vowels appear together, the sound produced is usually that of the first vowel. This mnemonic rhyme can help you to remember this rule:

> When two vowels go walking,
> The first does the talking.

The most common double vowels are e and o, as in:

tr**ee**   thr**ee**   p**ee**l   p**oo**l   p**oo**r   sch**oo**l

You don't get many English words spelt with aa, ii or uu. But of course there are some, mostly from other languages:

aa   aah   aardvark   bazaar   naan   salaam

ii   radii   skiing

uu   continuum   vacuum

The table on pages 16–17 contains a list of words you should easily be able to spell. They all have long vowel sounds mostly made by the silent e *or* a combination of vowels.

Long a sounds	Long e sounds	Long i sounds	Long o sounds	Long u sounds
aid	beam	bike	boast	argue
air	bean	bite	boat	beauty
ape	bee	chime	bone	cube
ate	beef	cry	boot	cue
baby	creep	dial	broke	cute
bail	dear	die	chose	due
bane	deer	dine	close	dune
cake	deep	dive	coat	fuel
came	ear	drive	cone	fume
cane	eel	file	dome	fury
care	feel	fire	dose	fuse
chain	feet	five	door	hue
chair	flea	fly	drove	huge
clay	free	glide	foam	June
crayon	gear	grime	goat	mule
dairy	green	hide	hoe	mute
dame	greet	hike	hole	puke
dare	heal	hire	home	pure
day	heel	hive	hope	rescue
decay	heap	kite	hose	rude
face	here	lime	joke	rue
fail	jeep	line	lone	sue
fair	knee	live	mole	suit
fairy	lead	mile	nose	sure
fate	leap	mine	note	tube
gain	leaves	nine	pole	tune
game	meal	pie	pose	use
gate	mean	pile	road	value
glare	meat	pipe	rode	you
grade	meet	pride	roast	
hail	meek	prize	rose	
hate	neat	rice	smoke	
hay	needle	ride	soap	
lake	peach	side	stone	
lane	peal	slide	store	

➤

Long a sounds	Long e sounds	Long i sounds	Long o sounds
made	peer	smile	stove
mail	please	tie	those
main	queen	tire	toad
make	read	try	toast
nail	reed	while	toe
name	sea	white	tone
pail	seat	wire	vote
pair	seed	wise	
plain	sheep		
plane	sleep		
play	spear		
rain	tea		
rake	teacher		
ray	these		
sail	three		
save	tree		
say	weak		
stay	weed		
tail	wheat		
take			
train			
tray			
way			
wait			
whale			

Exercise 3

Use the table of words with long vowel sounds and your general knowledge to complete the activities.

a. Write down five words with a long a sound that have the following vowel combinations.

ai, ay, a with a silent e

b. Copy these words and fill in ai or ay to spell them correctly.

f _ _ r, sl _ _, r_ _ n, _ _ r, s _ _, tr _ _, w _ _ t, h _ _ r, pl _ _

c. Copy these words and fill in i or y to spell them correctly.

fl _, cr _ stal, ox _ gen, fla _ r, h _ mn, h _ m, pla _ ground, m _ stery, wh _ le, pr _ de

d. Copy each word on the left and underline the letters that make the long vowel sound.

Then choose the correct meaning and write it beside each word.

1. brave	fearless	fearful
2. choose	pick one	choice
3. dear	animal	precious
4. pale	light in colour	bucket
5. rice	stand up	starchy food
6. teach	show how to	explain
7. huge	very big	put your arms round
8. real	genuine	round part of fishing rod
9. clean	not dirty	see-through

e. Find at least ten words with each of the following letter combinations. Try to find words that are not in the list on pages 16–17.

ee, ea, ie, ai

Vowel and consonant combinations

Some combinations of a vowel and a consonant can make a new, long vowel sound.

The vowel sound aw: The sound aw, as in saw, can be spelt in different ways:

aw – draw, saw   au – August, because   augh – naughty   ough – thought

Word list

aw	au	augh	ough
awful	August	taught	bought
draw	author	naughty	nought
drawing	autumn		thought
law	because		
lawyer	cause		
saw	dinosaur		
withdraw	exhaust		
	fault		
	haunt		
	laundry		
	saucer		

Exercise 4

a. **The missing sound in each word is aw but it can be spelt in different ways. Copy the sentences and fill in the correct letters to make the sound.**

It is not my f_ _lt.

My brother likes to dr_ _ pictures.

It is against the l_ _ to steal.

_ _tumn is my favourite season.

My little sister is very n_ _ghty.

I like school bec_ _se I learn a lot.

b. **These words all have the vowel sound aw but some of them are spelt incorrectly.**

Find the words that are spelt incorrectly.

Rewrite them using the correct letters (aw, au, augh or ough) to spell the words correctly.

Awgust, auful, lawndry, because, sawcer, hawnted, applaws, thawtful, dinosawr

The vowel sound ow: The vowel sound ow, as in cow, can be spelt in two different ways:

ow – cow, how, now   ou – noun, our, out

Word list

ow	ou
allow	about
bow	account
clown	amount
cow	bound
coward	cloud
crowd	council
crown	count
flower	doubt
growl	found
how	mountain
however	noun
owl	out
power	pronoun
powder	pronounce
shower	round
towel	sound
tower	without

Exercise 5

a. **Find a word in the word list above to match each definition. Write the word and make sure you can spell it correctly.**

bird with large eyes

cloth used to dry yourself

high building

white shape in the sky

work out how many there are

very high rocky hill

part of speech, also called a naming word

noise

permit to do something

➤

b. Find ten words with the long vowel sound ow in this wordsearch.

A	J	P	O	U	N	D	G	C
B	T	O	O	C	U	A	H	L
C	O	W	A	R	D	B	F	O
D	W	E	P	O	V	C	O	W
E	E	R	O	W	W	D	U	N
F	L	O	U	D	X	D	N	M
G	L	M	Q	S	Y	E	D	K
H	O	W	E	V	E	R	I	L
I	K	N	R	T	Z	F	J	P

Do you remember?

When a word has two or more syllables, it may contain two or more vowel sounds.

The vowel sound ar: The vowel sound ar, as in car, is usually spelt ar.

One exception is the root word 'heart'.

Word list			
apart	carbon	mark	remark
arm	cart	market	sharp
army	dark	pardon	star
art	garden	part	tar
bar	harbour	partner	
bargain	hard	party	
car	lard	regard	

Exercise 6

a. Each of these words has an extra letter in it. Find the extra letter and write the word correctly.

cairbon, harboiur, haerd, ciart, marik, mearket, peardon, paert, dairk, gayrden, laerd, plartner, pearty

b. Use a word from the word list on page 21 to answer each question.

What is the black stuff on the road?

Where does your mother plant vegetables?

Where do the boats sail from?

What vehicle does the horse pull?

What vehicle runs on petrol?

What is the opposite of soft?

What is the opposite of light?

c. Use the following words in sentences to show their meanings.

bargain, market, pardon, remark, heart

The vowel sound er: The vowel sound er, as in her, can be spelt in different ways:

er – after, her   ir – bird, dirt   ear – early, earth

Word list				
er			**ir**	**ear**
adverb	inner	paper	bird	early
after	joker	pepper	birth	earth
baker	kerb	perfect	circle	search
beaker	ladder	person	dirty	
boxer	liver	river	giraffe	
camper	matter	ruler	girl	
certain	member	servant	skirt	
chapter	meter	service	shirt	
climber	mercy	shower	thirst	
danger	mermaid	thermometer	whirl	
fertile	mother	tiger		
fever	nerve	water		
hammer	never	whisper		
her	other	youngster		
herd	over			

Exercise 7

The vowel sound er is missing from these words. Choose the correct letters, er, ir or ear, and write the words correctly.

b _ d, aft _, th _ st, box _, c _ cle, hamm _, s _ ch, h _, g _ l, k _ b, m _ maid, moth _, d _ ty, riv _, _ ly, tig _, wat _, _ th

The vowel sound or: The vowel sound or, as in for, can be spelt in different ways:

or – for	ar – war
orr – borrow	arr – quarrel

Word list

or		orr	ar	arr
acorn	orange	borrow	award	quarrel
border	ordinary	correct	quart	quarry
corn	organ	correction	quarter	warrior
corner	origin	corrupt	reward	
forbid	pore	porridge	towards	
form	report	sorrow	war	
former	short	sorry	ward	
fortune	sort	tomorrow	warm	
forward	story			
glory	support			
lord	tornado			
moral	torture			
normal				

Exercise 8

a. The vowel sound or is missing from these words. Choose the correct letters, or, orr, ar or arr, and write to spell the words correctly.

qu _ ter, c _ n, f _ m, c _ ect, c _ d, n _ mal, _ ange, s _ y, rep _ t, sh _ t, w _ , w _ ior

b. These words with the long vowel sound or are spelt incorrectly. Write the correct spelling of each word.

acarn, farrbid, glorry, orrgan, porr, barow, parridge, tarrnado, tomorow, rewarrd, worrm, quorrel

The 'i before e' rule

The long vowel sound ee causes many spelling problems because it can be spelt ei or ie.

The 'i before e except after c' rule is one of the best known spelling rules. But, that is just part of the rule. You need to remember the whole rule if you are going to use it to spell better.

Do you remember?

Use i before e,

except after c,

when the sound is ee.

If ay is the sound

It's the other way round!

Word list			
i before e when the sound is ee		**except after c**	**When the sound is ay use ei**
achieve	niece	ceiling	eight
believe	piece	deceive	heir
brief	pierce	receipt	feint
chief	priest	receive	freight
field	relief		neighbour
fierce	shield		reign
grief	thief		vein
hygiene	yield		weigh
			weight

Exceptions to the rule: As with all the spelling rules, there are exceptions to this rule.

Word list	
i before e after c	**e before i**
ancient	either
conscience	neither
efficient	seize
science	weird
society	
species	
sufficient	

Exercise 9

a. Choose ei or ie and write these words correctly.

fr _ _ nd, _ _ ghteen, s _ _ ge, v _ _ n, f _ _ ld, r_ _ gn, cash _ _ r, rec _ _ pt, rel _ _ f, dec _ _ t, f _ _ rce, v _ _ l

b. Proofread the following sentences. Rewrite correctly any sentences with spelling mistakes.

It is better to give than to recieve.

What you beleive you will achieve.

Love your freinds and nieghbours like yourself.

That boat leaks like a sieve.

Niether a borrower nor a lender be.

All things grow with time, except greif.

Expereince is the mother of wisdom.

Patience is a virtue.

Vareity is the spice of life.

c. Find the correctly spelt word in each pair.

1. believe	beleive	**6.** forfeit	forfiet
2. acheive	achieve	**7.** freind	friend
3. recieve	receive	**8.** science	sceince
4. either	iether	**9.** niece	neice
5. seize	sieze		

d. Write a sentence to show the meaning of each of these words:

friend, fiend, piece, peace

2. Consonant sounds

As with vowels, consonant sounds can be spelt in different ways. The consonants c and g are also pronounced differently depending on which letter follows them. Listening to consonant sounds can help you improve your spelling.

The k sound

The k sound, as in kill, can be spelt in different ways:

c – cat, can, car, action

cc – account, accurate

ch – school, chemist

ck – back, duck, pack

k – king, kitten, kite

qu – queen, bouquet (the kw sound is *always* spelt qu)

que – antique, unique

If the k sound is followed by the vowels e or i, then the word is normally spelt with a k. For example:

ketchup   key   kite   kitten

If the k sound is followed by a consonant or the vowels a, o or u, then the word is normally spelt with a c. For example:

cat   cape   core   computer   cut   cute   climb   crumb   crust

If the k sound is at the end of a syllable with a short vowel sound, then it is normally spelt ck. For example:

back   clock   duck   flick   luck   tickle   wicket

Some words from other languages are exceptions to these rules:

Kangaroo, kookaburra and kung-fu don't obey the c or k rule.

Yak (the animal) doesn't end with ck.

Word list

c sounds like k

cab	clutter	crime
call	coat	crust
camel	code	cry
can	cone	cube
cat	cope	cucumber
catch	crash	cut
caterpillar	crayon	cute
climb		

k sounds like k

kangaroo	kid
keen	kind
keep	king
kennel	kiss
kettle	kitchen
key	kite
keyboard	kitten
kick	

➤

ck sounds like k

back	flock	pick	slack
black	jacket	quack	slick
chicken	lick	quick	smack
check	luck	rack	stack
clock	mock	rock	stick
cricket	muck	rocket	tick
deck	nick	sack	wick
dock	pack	sick	wreck
flick	peck	suck	

Exercise 10

a. **Copy these words and fill in c or k to spell them correctly.**

_ at, _ ing, ba _ e, _ a _ e, ma _ e, _ ame, _ ane, _ laim, _ ettle, _ ey, _ ingfisher, _ rayon, _ ute

b. **Choose the correct word from the ones in the brackets.**

Our garden is at the (bake / back) of our house.

The kittens are very (cute / cube).

I boiled some water in the (kennel / kettle).

I wished him good (lick / luck) for the test.

There is a worm under that (rock / rocket).

c. **Unscramble these words to make words with a k sound.**

tchac, naec, cikt, ttiken, csuk, locck, cqauk, ricem, umberccu, lacem, siks, nigk

---

Word list

ch sounds like k

ache	chorus	psychology
anchor	chrome	scheme
chameleon	chrysanthemum	schedule
chemist	echo	school
Christian	mechanic	stomach
Christmas	orchid	

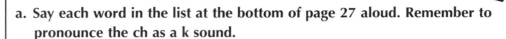

Exercise 11

a. **Say each word in the list at the bottom of page 27 aloud. Remember to pronounce the ch as a k sound.**

b. **List any words you don't know. Use a dictionary to find out what each word means.**

c. **Learn to spell these words using the method you find easiest.**

The sounds of c and g

You've just learnt that the letter c can make a **hard** sound like a k in words such as cat, camel and climb.

The letter c can also make a **soft** sound like an s when it comes before an e, i or y. You can hear this in words such as cell, city, ice and cycle.

The letter g makes a **hard** sound when it comes before an a, o or u. You can hear this in words such as game, go and gun.

It has a **soft** sound like a j when it comes before an e, i or y. You can hear this sound in words such as germ, ginger and gym.

Word list				
cinema	carpet	germ	giraffe	voice
celery	certain	legend	good	college
cider	face	age	garden	gem
corn	dance	logic	gum	grim
cucumber	decent	gentle	cry	girl
camel	notice	ginger	gull	grin
brace	pace	large	price	gold
ace	mice	cabbage	rice	original
agent	peace	rag	science	
cancel	ocean	gutter	trace	
centre	cute	going	twice	

Exercise 12

a. **Find all the words in the list above with a c sound.**

b. **Identify all the words with a g sound. Note that some of the words have both a c sound and a g sound.**

c. Copy and complete this table to sort the words into hard and soft sounds. Write your words in alphabetical order in the table. Note that some of the words will appear in more than one column.

Hard c sound (like a k)	Soft c sound (like an s)	Hard g sound (like a g)	Soft g sound (like a j)

d. Make sure you can spell all the words in the list. Use the 'Copy – Say – Test – Correct' method to test yourself.

Other j sounds

You've seen that the letter g can make a soft j sound when it is followed by e, i or y.

When the j sound is followed by an a, o or u, the word is normally spelt with a j. For example:

jam   jog   joke   juice

When the j sound comes after a short vowel sound, the word is normally spelt with dge. For example:

edge   judge   ridge

There are no English words with a double j.

Word list

jack	jog	bridge	judge
jacket	jug	budget	nudge
jam	jump	dodge	ridge
jar	junk	edge	smudge
job	just	gadget	wedge

Exercise 13

a. Join the beginnings with the ending -dge to make eight words. The first one has been done for you.

he + dge = hedge   ba + dge =   smu + dge =

do + dge =   e + dge =   ju + dge =

nu + dge =   ri + dge =

b. Choose g or j and write these words correctly.

_ em, _ lue, _ ump, _ acket, _ uice, _ lum

The ch sound

When the ch sound comes after a short vowel it is spelt tch. For example:

itch   kitchen   patch   witch

The tch spelling is *never* found at the beginning of a word.

Exceptions to this short vowel rule are:

attach   much   ostrich   rich   sandwich   such   which

In most other words the ch sound is spelt ch. For example:

children   church   chicken   touch

Word list			
chilly	match	chin	watch
teacher	chew	hatch	branch
pitch	search	chair	change
champion	watch	chimpanzee	cheese
church	beach	chip	cheetah
chain	kitchen	march	chase
catch	channel	chalk	chatter
cheat	check	child	cheap

Exercise 14

a. Say each word from the word list above aloud. Underline the letters that make the ch sound.

b. Choose one word from the list to match each definition.

A person who shows the class what to do

The fastest of the large wild cats

The sticks that you use to write on a chalkboard

The item you wear that tells you time

A young member of a family

A sandy place next to the sea

What you sit on

What you do to food before you swallow it

c. Use the list and your dictionary to find five words that start with ch in each of the following groups:

animals   types of food

The s sound

The s sound that you hear in the word sick, can be spelt in different ways:

s – sail, sand, snake   ss – hiss, loss, pass
sc – scent, scratch, scream   ce – once, since, ounce

The single s is normally used at the start of a word, or to make a word plural.

The double ss is generally used when the s sound follows a short vowel sound that is stressed.

In most other words with an s sound in them, the soft c (ce, ci, or cy) is used. Exceptions are bus, plus and us, where the s sound is spelt with a single s.

The z sound

When an s comes between two vowels in a word, it sounds like a z. For example:

daisy   fuse   use

If the z sound comes at the end of a word, the s is not doubled. For example:

as   is   has   his   was

Words never end with a single z.

If the z sound follows a short vowel, spell the word with zz. For example:

buzz   fizz   whizz

If the z sound follows a long vowel or a combination of vowels, use ze. For example:

freeze   laze   ooze

You will deal with plurals using s and es in the next chapter.

Word list

s sound spelt with single s	s sound spelt with double ss	s sound spelt sc	z sound spelt with double zz
sad	ass	fascinate	blizzard
safety	assist	muscle	buzz
salt	bass	scene	dazzle
same	bless	scent	dizzy
sausage	blossom	science	fizz
seat	boss	scissors	fuzzy
secret	chess		jazz
see	class	**s sounds like z**	nozzle
sell	cross	**but spelt se**	puzzle
sentence	dress	because	sizzle
separate	essay	browse	
sign	fuss	bruise	**z sound spelt**
silly	glasses	cheese	**with ze**
silver	grass	choose	breeze
simple	guess	disease	freeze
sister	harmless	ease	gauze
skeleton	hiss	lose	ooze
sleep	kiss	noise	seize
smile	lass	pause	sneeze
snake	less	please	snooze
soccer	loss	tease	squeeze
social	mass	whose	
song	massive		
soon	mess		
sport	message		
subject	miss		
suddenly	moss		
super	pass		
supper	passage		
swim	press		
syllable	stress		
system	toss		
	vessel		
	wilderness		

Exercise 15

a. Copy and complete these words by filling in **se** or **ze** at the end.

fu _ _, becau _ _, chee _ _, lo _ _, sei _ _, choo _ _, snoo _ _, oo _ _, free _ _, noi _ _, plea _ _

b. Copy these words and circle the ones that are spelt correctly. Put a cross through the words that are spelt incorrectly.

bussing, hizzing, fizzy, missing, kizzing, mizz, acrozz, class, pissa, pussle, exprezz, buss, passing, mazzive, carelezz, across, drezz, blissard, message

c. Write the correct spelling for each incorrect word in (b).

d. Unscramble the letters to make correctly spelt words with the s sound spelt **sc**.

enecs, sincatfae, clesum, ccinsee, ssssorci

e. Find a word with a double **ss** spelling to complete each sentence.

Excuse me, could you _____ me?

I can't see so well, so I have to wear _____.

The pupils in my _____ are all good at spelling.

I didn't know the answer so I had to _____.

I couldn't answer the phone, so he left a _____.

_____ this button to open the door.

I like to go camping in the _____.

The f sound

The f sound as in fall can be spelt in different ways:

f – fall, frog, frown   ff – off, puff
ph – elephant, graph, pharmacy   ugh – enough, laugh

No words start with ff or ugh.

Use ff at the end of a word if the f sound follows a short vowel sound. For example:

bluff   stuff

If the sound is in the middle of a word, use ff if the sound is between two syllables. For example:

fluffy   waffle

Use the single f if the sound follows a long vowel sound (including words with the silent e) or if the word ends with the ft sound. For example:

beef   life   lift

Learn to recognise the words that are spelt with ph and ugh for the f sound.

Word list			
f spelt f	**f spelt ff**	**f spelt ph**	**f spelt ugh**
Many words use a	affect	alphabet	cough
single f.	baffle	aphid	enough
	bluff	dolphin	laugh
	buffalo	elephant	rough
	cliff	geography	tough
	coffee	graph	trough
	differ	hyphen	
	difference	microphone	
	difficult	nephew	
	effect	orphan	
	effort	pharaoh	
	fluffy	pharmacy	
	giraffe	phone	
	huff	photo	
	off	physical	
	offend	physics	
	office	prophet	
	raffle	sphere	
	scruffy	telephone	
	sniff	trophy	
	staff		
	stiff		
	stuff		
	suffer		
	toffee		
	traffic		
	waffle		

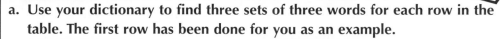

Exercise 16

a. Use your dictionary to find three sets of three words for each row in the table. The first row has been done for you as an example.

Starts with	One syllable	Two syllables	More than two syllables
fa	far farm fat	farmer father fatter	fabulous faculty fashionable
fe			
fi			
fo			
fu			
fl			
fr			

b. These words with an f sound are all spelt incorrectly. Rewrite each one with the correct spelling for the f sound.

dwarffs, saffe, cofee, reffer, beeffy, phizzled, coff, enuff, eleffant, fluphy, snifed, stouph, supher, diference, buphalo, ephective, cofin, ffrom, thefft, graff

c. The blank spaces in each word represent an f sound. Choose ph or gh and write the words correctly.

cou _ _, rou _ _, ele _ _ ant, _ _ ysical, tou _ _, _ _ antom, tele _ _ one, lau _ _ ter, tro _ _ y, drau _ _ t, _ _ rase, ne _ _ ew, atmos _ _ ere, or _ _ an, pro _ _ et, geogra _ _ y, enou _ _, dol _ _ in

d. Learn to spell the words in the word list on page 34 using the method you find easiest.

Doubling consonants

Many words are spelt with double consonants. When you listen to words it can be difficult to tell whether the consonant is single or double. For example, in the words cat and cattle. There are some rules that can help you:

◆ For one syllable words that end with f, l, s and z, double the consonant at the end. For example: puff, pull, miss, buzz.

◆ If the consonant sound comes after a short vowel in the middle of a word, it is normally doubled.

◆ The consonants j, k, q, v, w and x are never doubled.

Exercise 17

a. **Say each word out loud. Choose the correct spelling in each pair based on the sound and the rules on page 35.**

1. stoped	stopped	**9.** flufy	fluffy
2. droped	dropped	**10.** buzing	buzzing
3. running	runing	**11.** hissing	hising
4. hiden	hidden	**12.** puling	pulling
5. shinning	shining	**13.** growing	growwing
6. beginning	begining	**14.** lovving	loving
7. spining	spinning	**15.** lackking	lacking
8. faling	falling		

b. **Make your own spelling list of ten words with a double consonant that you find difficult to remember.**

c. **Use the spelling method you find easiest to learn to spell these words.**

Do you remember?

Revise the phonics rules and then complete the following exercises.

Exercise 18

a. **Find the word that sounds different in each group.**

1. cash	wash	crash	dash
2. grand	wander	panda	gander
3. wand	band	stand	land
4. batch	match	latch	watch
5. chill	will	thrill	child
6. loud	proud	wound	pound

b. **Choose the correct spelling in each pair.**

1. seet	seat		**8.** clauw	claw
2. holiday	holidai		**9.** sorcer	saucer
3. windauw	window		**10.** loud	lowd
4. throo	threw		**11.** fewd	food
5. poosh	push		**12.** enjoied	enjoyed
6. paynt	paint		**13.** cirly	curly
7. poynt	point		**14.** cleer	clear

c. **List the correctly spelt words from (b) in alphabetical order. Circle the vowel sound or sounds in each word.**

d. **Write down five words with each of the following sounds and spellings.**

c as in cat	ee as in ear	f as in fair	z as in fuse
eh as in bread	c as in cell	f as in laugh	
ur as in fur	s as in sugar	tt as in cattle	

Structural rules

You have already learnt that there are many rules for spelling in English. In this chapter you are going to learn the rules for making plurals and for adding prefixes and suffixes to root words. As with the phonetic spelling rules, there are always some words that are exceptions to the rules.

1. Rules for making plurals

Do you remember?

◆ Nouns name people, places and things.

◆ Nouns can be singular or plural.

◆ A singular noun is one person, place or thing. A plural noun is more than one person, place or thing.

◆ When singular nouns become plural they change their spelling to show the change in their meaning. How they change depends on what letter is at the end of the singular noun.

Making plurals by adding s

You can add an s to most nouns to form plurals.

Word list			
dog	garden	tree	stick
house	broom	eye	paper
school	key	friend	bicycle
door	mother	duck	kitchen
car	place	horse	bedroom
head	window	rabbit	train
king	book	plant	boy
town	girl	dragon	father

Exercise 1

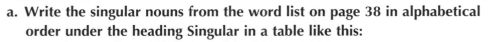

a. **Write the singular nouns from the word list on page 38 in alphabetical order under the heading Singular in a table like this:**

Singular	Plural	Singular	Plural
bedroom	bedrooms	bicycle	bicycles

b. **Write the plural of each singular noun in the table.**

c. **Write sentences that use the plural forms of each set of words.**

    1. farm, cow, bull

    2. garage, boy, car

    3. hospital, girl, present

    4. home, parent, tree

    5. zoo, monkey, cage

d. **Rewrite each sentence changing all the nouns to plural forms. You may need to change or delete some of the words in the sentences.**

The crazy ape threw a stick and stone at the onlooker.

The pretty tin was decorated with a colourful button and a silver bead.

The energetic boy jumped across the stream.

The rowdy girl cheered and danced to encourage the athlete.

The winner of the race received a gold medal.

Making plurals by adding es

If the noun ends with a ch, sh, ss, s, x or z, add es to make the plural.

Word list			
boss	church	gas	princess
box	dish	hutch	sandwich
bus	dress	lioness	waltz
bush	fox	match	wish
circus	glass	patch	witness

Exercise 2

a. Copy and complete the following:

one church, many _____   one sandwich, many _____

one circus, many _____   one hutch, many _____

one lioness, many _____   one waltz, many _____

one match, many _____   one wish, many _____

one glass, many _____   one gas, many _____

b. Copy the puzzle into your book. Complete these clues using words from the list on page 39 and then write them in the puzzle using their plural form.

Down

1. A _____ is a container used for objects.

2. A _____ is a sly animal.

3. A _____ is a serving bowl.

4. A _____ is a plant.

5. A _____ is a feminine piece of clothing.

6. A _____ is a form of transport.

Across

1. A _____ is a person in charge.

c. Write sentences that include the plural forms of each set of words.

   1. princess, castle, wand

   2. frog, patch, skin

   3. boss, worker, box

   4. car, tree, freeway

   5. witness, reporter, accident

Making plurals of words ending in y

To change a noun that ends in:

◆ a vowel + y to the plural, just add **s**

◆ a consonant + y to the plural, change the y to **i** and add **es**.

              vowel

              |

           boy – boys

           sky – skies

         consonant

Word list

alley	energy	lady	ray
assembly	fly	luxury	storey
baby	holiday	monkey	story
country	industry	party	summary
day	journey	play	trolley
donkey	key	puppy	turkey

Exercise 3

a. Copy and complete this table. Add all the words from the word list above.

Nouns ending in a vowel + y		Nouns ending in a consonant + y	
Singular	**Plural**	**Singular**	**Plural**
key	keys	puppy	puppies

b. **Rewrite these sentences using the plural form of the nouns. You may need to change or delete some of the words in the sentence.**

A young boy cannot join the army.

The lady found the book in the library.

I have a theory about why the girl does not play with the toy.

The monkey lived happily in the valley.

The deputy investigated the robbery.

c. **Change each noun from the plural to singular form.**

enemies, spies, strawberries, companies, galleries, flies, poppies

Making plurals of words ending in an f sound

To change most nouns ending in f or fe to the plural, change f or fe to **ves**.

To change a few nouns ending in f or fe to the plural, just add **s**.

A few plural nouns can end in either **fs** or **ves**.

Word list

f changes to ves		Add s only	Can be spelt with
			s or ves
calf – calves	loaf – loaves	chief – chiefs	hoof – hoofs or hooves
life – lives	shelf – shelves	cliff – cliffs	scarf – scarfs or scarves
half – halves	thief – thieves	belief–beliefs	wharf – wharfs or
knife – knives	wife – wives	reef – reefs	wharves
leaf – leaves	wolf – wolves	roof – roofs	

Exercise 4

a. **Copy and complete this list.**

one loaf	several _____
a _____	four hooves
the wolf	many _____
one _____	two scarfs
a thief	two _____

the chief	three _____
one life	nine _____
a _____	many beliefs
one shelf	four _____
the reef	several _____

b. Use a dictionary to help you write the plural form of these words.

dwarf, elf, self, sheaf

c. Write plural nouns that mean:

married women, baby cows, sharp utensils, landing places for ships

d. Rewrite these sentences and correct the mistakes.

After I cut ten apples in half, I had twenty halfs.

Gang of thiefs steal cars in our neighbourhoodes.

The rooves of the houses were damaged during the hurricane.

The ladys found the cliff's steep and difficult to climb.

The leafs fell from the branchs.

Making plurals of words ending in o

To change most nouns that end in an o to the plural, add **es**.

To change the following nouns that end in o to the plural, add **s**:

◆ nouns that end in oo, for example: zoos

◆ musical words ending in o, for example: cellos

◆ a noun ending in a vowel and an o, for example: radios

Some plural nouns can end in **os** or **oes**, for example: mottos or mottoes.

Word list

Plural spelt with es	Plural spelt with s	Plural can be spelt with s or es
buffaloes	banjos	halos or haloes
cargoes	cellos	mangos or mangoes
dominoes	curios	mementos or mementoes
echoes	igloos	mottos or mottoes
heroes	kilos	zeros or zeroes
mosquitoes	patios	
potatoes	pianos	
tomatoes	photos	
tornadoes	radios	
volcanoes	solos	
	studios	
	zoos	

Exercise 5

a. Write both the singular and plural forms of each noun in the list above.

b. Use the rules and a dictionary to help you write the plural form of these words and then use them in sentences which show that you understand their meaning.

   video, concerto, tattoo, avocado, rodeo

c. Rewrite these sentences using the plural form of the nouns. You may need to change or delete some of the words in the sentence.

   The bellow of the buffalo scared the mosquito.

   A tornado damaged the crop of potato, tomato and mango.

   The talented musician played the piano, cello and banjo.

   I display a curio and memento from the trip in my studio.

   I wonder if an Eskimo hangs a photo on the wall of the igloo.

d. Copy and complete the sentences using plural nouns from the list above.

   The _____ rang out across the valley.

   They always built _____ around the houses they bought so they could sit outside and enjoy the view.

   _____ is a fun game to play.

   I feel sad when I see animals in cages at _____.

   Motorists listen to programmes broadcast on the _____ in their cars.

Exceptions to the rules

Some nouns do not follow the rules:

◆ Some plural nouns stay the same as the singular, for example: sheep – sheep.

◆ Some plural nouns change their spelling, for example: mouse – mice.

◆ Some words are always plural, for example: police.

Word list

Same singular and plural forms	Change spelling in the plural	Only used in the plural form	
aircraft	child – children	barracks	pants
baggage	die – dice	cattle	pliers
bread	foot – feet	clothes	pyjamas
buck	goose –geese	goods	savings
deer	louse – lice	headquarters	scissors
fish	man – men	mathematics	species
moose	ox – oxen	measles	trousers
reindeer	tooth – teeth	news	tweezers
series	woman – women		

Exercise 6

a. Copy and complete this list.

one die	several _____
an aircraft	four _____
the _____	many cattle
one _____	two geese
a man	two _____
the child	three _____
one ox	nine _____
a buck	many _____
one pair of _____	four pairs of scissors
one pair of _____	five pairs of trousers

b. Find plural nouns from the word list on page 45 to match these clues.

hand tools used to grip something

small plucking instruments

insects that live on humans and animals

numbered cubes used in games

buildings where soldiers stay

c. Choose nouns from the word list on page 45 to complete these sentences. Remember to use the correct form of the noun.

They tapped their _____ to the music.

There are millions of _____ in the sea.

I had one _____ pulled out when I went to the dentist to have my _____ checked.

None of my _____ arrived at the airport so I had to buy new _____ to wear.

There was only one piece of _____ that I found interesting in the news broadcast.

Making plurals of foreign words

Many English words are from other languages. These words often follow the rules of their origins.

To change a noun that ends in:

◆ -us to the plural, add **es** or **i**.

◆ -eau to the plural, add **x** or **s**.

◆ -a to the plural, add **e**.

◆ -is to the plural, change -is to **-es**.

Word list

Nouns ending in -us

cactus – cactuses or cacti
hippopotamus – hippopotamuses or hippopotami
octopus – octopuses
syllabus – syllabuses or syllabi

Nouns ending in -eau

bureau – bureaux or bureaus
plateau – plateaux or plateaus
tableau – tableaux or tableaus

Nouns ending in -a

antenna – antennae
formula – formulae
larva – larvae
vertebra – vertebrae

Nouns ending in -is

axis – axes
crisis – crises
oasis – oases
thesis – theses

Exercise 7

a. **Rewrite each rule on page 46 using your own words and list three matching examples from the word list.**

For example:

Add e to form the plural of nouns ending in a.

formula – formulae

larva – larvae

vertebra – vertebrae

b. **Use the rules and a dictionary to help you write the plural form of these words and then use them in sentences which show that you understand their meaning.**

parenthesis, focus, beau, alga

Making plurals of compound words

Do you remember?

◆ A compound word is made up of two or more words joined together.

◆ Some compound words have hyphens.

◆ Examples of compound words: cookbook, mother-in-law

47

To change most compound words *without* a hyphen to the plural, change the last word to the plural form. For example:

cookbook – cookbook**s**.

To change a compound word *with* a hyphen to a plural, change the main noun part to the plural form. For example:

mother-in-law – mother**s**-in-law

Word list

backpack	pancake	daughter-in-law	looker-on
boyfriend	rainbow	lady-in-waiting	maid-of-honour
campfire	spoonful	runner-up	father-in-law
churchyard	stepfather	passer-by	sister-in-law
keyboard	stepmother	editor-in-chief	
notebook	wheelchair		

Exercise 8

a. **Use the rules to help you write the plural form of each word in the word list above.**

b. **Form compound words by matching a word in column A to a word in column B below. Write the plural form of each compound word you make.**

Set your answers out like this:

water + melon = watermelon → watermelons

Column A	Column B
water	mint
foot	ball
week	mother
pepper	board
butter	melon
sun	end
base	man
pine	print
grand	flower
black	apple
gentle	fly

➤

c. **Unscramble these compound nouns to spell them correctly. The capital letter is the first letter in the word.**

Ssnowin-a-l, arydhCchrus, puun-Rnres, rleseCeaehrd, sAoeotfnnr

d. **Which new words come from these pairs of words? Write the compound word and its plural form, if one exists.**

helicopter + port = heliport → heliports

motor + hotel   breakfast + lunch

cheese + burger   international + police

e. **Make up five new compound words of your own. Write them like this:**

_____ + _____ = _____ → _____ (plural)

Do you remember?

Revise the rules for making plurals and then complete the following exercises.

Exercise 9

a. **Change the following words to plurals.**

mother	book	formula	waltz
church	dish	octopus	turkey
party	baby	ox	chief
loaf	thief	piano	potato
echo	zoo	belief	tooth
child	louse	play	plateau
scissors	trousers	bus	son-in-law
axis	runner-up	fox	boss

b. **Rewrite the sentences using plural forms of the nouns.**

The police conducted a search for the thief in the bush near our house.

The man strummed a tune on his banjo.

The child played the piano at the music concert.

The deer in the country eats a leaf from a tree.

A mouse gnawed the corner of the photo of my hero.

c. Write a sentence using each set of words in their plural form.

kangaroo, lioness, show

lady, monkey, loaf

journey, dwarf, radio

mango, baggage, hippopotamus

passer-by, crisis, churchyard

d. Copy and complete these sentences using the plural form of the nouns in brackets.

Many sly (fox) hide behind (bush) and spy on (hen) laying (egg).

The (girl) wore (pyjamas) to the (party).

The (woman) received (medal) because they were the (runner-up) in the (competition).

The (bookshelf) were loaded with (book), (curio), (photograph) and (memento).

All the (woman) baked (loaf) of bread to give to the many poor (person).

e. Write the plural of each word.

buffalo	wolf	cockatoo	fork
pony	mouse	wife	shoe
monkey	goose	loaf of bread	shampoo
ox	mosquito	potato	toothbrush
fox	ass	knife	dove

2. Rules for adding prefixes and suffixes

Do you remember?

A **root** is the basic word from which other words are formed. For example:

*joy*ous, en*joy*ment, over*joy*ed.

You can change the meaning of the root word by adding letters before or after it. The letters you add on are called **affixes**. There are two kinds of affixes: prefixes and suffixes.

A **prefix** is a group of letters that are added to the front of the root word. For example: *en*joy.

Prefixes have a definite meaning. If you know the meaning of and how to spell the common prefixes, it can help you work out the meaning and spelling of many words.

A **suffix** is a group of letters that are added after the root word. Some suffixes begin with a vowel and others with a consonant. For example: overjoy*ed*, joy*ful*.

Suffixes have a definite function and often indicate a part of speech.

Prefixes

The spelling of the rest of the word does not change when you add a prefix to it. This is true even when the last letter of the prefix and the first letter of the word are the same:

mis + spell = misspell

dis + solve = dissolve

il + legal = illegal

Exceptions to this rule include 'all' and 'well'. For the exceptions to the rule you only add one l:

all + right = alright

well + come = welcome

Read and learn how to spell the words in the third column of this list.

Word list		
Prefix	**Meaning**	**Examples**
aero	air	aerobics, aeroplane, aerosol
ante	before	antenatal, ante meridiem
anti	against	anticlimax, anticlockwise, antiseptic
de	away, down, removing	de-stress, descend, defrost
dis	not, apart	dishonest, disbelief, disarm
il, im, in, ir	not	illegal, impossible, inexpensive, irregular
mis	wrong	misuse, misunderstood
pre	before, in front	prefix, precaution, premature
pro	supporting, onwards	pro-government, proceed
un	not	unhappy, unimportant, unreliable
uni	one	unicorn, uniform, unison
bi	two	biathlon, bicycle, binocular
tri	three	triangle, tricolour, tricycle

Exercise 10

a. Find the word that is spelt correctly in each pair.

   1. altogether   alltogether   **6.** procaution   precaution

   2. ilogical   illogical   **7.** insatisfied   dissatisfied

   3. wellfare   welfare   **8.** inexpensive unexpensive

   4. iregular   irregular   **9.** unpleased   displeased

   5. preceed   proceed   **10.** inpossible   impossible

b. What does each of these prefixes mean? Use the word list and your dictionary to help you.

detach, **anti**biotic, **un**inspired, **tri**pod, **aero**batics, **multi**racial, **post**pone, **semi**circle, **tele**vision, **trans**port

c. Correct these sentences. Use the rules, the word list and your dictionary to help you.

The hunchback of Notre Dame was mishapen.

The missprint in the advertisement led to confusion.

I was dissappointed with my spelling mark.

His misshap made him miss the race.

It is ilegal to smoke on the school grounds.

He went to hospital because his heart rate was iregular.

If you mispell ilogical I will know you did not learn your spelling words for the test.

Disolve the tablet in water.

Although James and Matthew are brothers, they are quite disimilar.

Do not unerve me by watching my every move.

d. What is the root word in each of these words?

discover, multicoloured, disagree, antisocial, unhappy, displeased, recoverable, understanding

Using prefixes to make opposites

You can put the prefixes **im-**, **in-**, **ir-**, **il-,** **dis-**, **un-**, **mis-** and **de-** in front of words to make them mean the opposite.

Word list

mobile – immobile	appearance – disappearance
perfect – imperfect	like – dislike
polite – impolite	
	kind – unkind
correct – incorrect	fortunately – unfortunately
direct – indirect	
attentive – inattentive	understood – misunderstood
finite – infinite	interpret – misinterpret
complete – incomplete	represent – misrepresent
convenient – inconvenient	
	accelerate – decelerate
rational – irrational	
literate – illiterate	

Exercise 11

a. **Use the method you find easiest to learn to spell any words in the list on page 53 that you are not sure of.**

b. **Add a prefix to each of these words to give them the opposite meaning.**

   accurate, capable, legal, regular, possible, probable, appear, rational, employed, fortune, patient, interested, involved, needed, understand, please

c. **These words are all incorrect. Change the prefixes to make them correct.**

   unmobile, inperfect, imcorrect, irdirect, ilattentive, disfinite, uncomplete, misconvenient

d. **How many words starting with in- can you list? Use five of the words in sentences that show you understand their meanings.**

Suffixes

Do you remember?

◆ Nouns name people, places and things.

◆ Adjectives describe nouns.

◆ Verbs are doing or action words.

◆ Adverbs describe verbs.

For example: The tall girl ran quickly.

When you add a suffix to a word it can change it from one part of speech to another. For example:

He is a <u>dream**er**</u> (noun).

I had a <u>dream**less**</u> (adjective) night.

I spent the night <u>dream**ing**</u> (verb) about my holiday.

He <u>dream**ily**</u> (adverb) stared at nothing.

These suffixes make nouns:

-er   -or   -ar   -hood   -ure   -ment   -age

These suffixes make adjectives:

-en -ish -less -ic -ous -ful -y

These suffixes make verbs:

-ing -ed -ure -en -ise -ize

The most common ending for adverbs is -ly.

Word list

Nouns	Adjectives	Verbs	Adverbs
actor	ambitious	begged	beautifully
beggar	beautiful	dramatise	bravely
fighter	heroic	fighting	generously
government	homeless	manufacture	happily
hostage	realistic	speaking	nervously
mixture	selfish	specialise	quickly
neighbourhood	windy	taxing	selfishly
singer	woollen		superbly

Exercise 12

a. Write two sentences. Both sentences must include a correctly spelt noun, adjective, verb and adverb from the word list above.

For example: The heroic hostage was speaking nervously.

b. Choose words from the word list above to complete the sentences.

The _____ scarf kept me warm.

The _____ child did not share.

The _____ beggar looked for shelter.

The famous _____ visited our _____.

The congregation gave _____ towards the collection.

c. Use your dictionary to help you change these:

1. verbs to nouns by adding the suffixes -er, -or or -ar

robbed, lied, waited, communicated, narrated

2. adjectives to adverbs by adding the suffix -ly

happy, smooth, false, rough, angry

3. nouns to adjectives by adding the suffix -ous

nerve, danger, joy, space, melody

4. adjectives to verbs by adding the suffix -en

sharp, wide, hard, soft, loose, light, weak, tight

d. Copy and complete the diagrams to change the verbs to nouns, adverbs and adjectives.

For example:

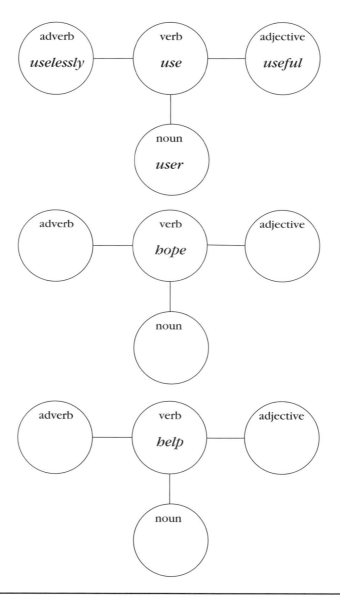

Now learn these rules to help you add suffixes correctly.

To add a suffix that begins with a consonant to a word that ends in a consonant, simply add the suffix:

govern + ment = government

| consonant |

To add a suffix that begins with a consonant to a word that ends in a vowel, simply add the suffix:

nice + ly = nicely

| vowel |

To add a suffix to a word that ends in a vowel + y, simply add the suffix:

delay + ed = delayed

| vowel |

To add a suffix to a word that ends in a consonant + y, change the y to an i:

rely + able = reliable

| consonant |

Exception: the suffix -ing does not obey this rule:

rely + ing = relying

Remember that the suffix -ful has only one l:

hope + ful = hopeful

There are *no* English words ending with full except for the word full.

Word list

Word ending in consonant + suffix beginning with consonant	Word ending in vowel + suffix	Word ending in vowel and y + suffix	Word ending in consonant and y, change y to i + suffix	Word ending in y + suffix -ing
government	nicely	delayed	rely – reliable	relying
madness	excitement	conveyed	heavy – heavily	conveying
gladness	likeable	destroyed	reply – replied	replying
helpful	advantageous	employment	empty – emptiness	emptying
wonderful	hopeful	enjoyment	beauty – beautiful	playing

57

Exercise 13

a. Write the root word and suffix of the following words.

For example: rely + able = reliable

heavily, replied, emptiness, supplier, carried

b. Revise the y rules and then copy and complete this table.

Verbs	+ ed	+ ing
study	studied	studying
marry		
copy		
pity		
obey		
enjoy		

c. Copy and complete these sentences with the suffix -ful or -fully.

I picked an arm_____ of beauti_____ flowers. My mother was wonder_____ happy when I gave them to her. Thank_____ she forgot my aw_____ punishment.

She greeted everyone cheer_____ while she walked the play_____ puppy.

He spoke truth_____ at the stress_____ hearing.

The boast_____ man bragged piti_____.

A spoon_____ of honey will hope_____ sweeten the bitter medicine.

d. Change these words into:

1. nouns by adding the suffix -ment

treat, replace, argue, move, settle

2. adjectives by adding the suffix -ful

use, spite, colour, care, grace

3. nouns by adding the suffix -ness

useful, spiteful, colourful, careful, gracious

e. Join these words and suffixes.

reply + ed = _____   reply + ing = _____

empty + ed = _____   empty + ing = _____

relay + ed = _____   relay + ing = _____

obey + ed = _____   obey + ing = _____

pity + ed = _____   pity + ing = _____

f. Rewrite this paragraph adding suitable suffixes to the words in brackets.

The (excite) children (hike) up the mountain without (notice) its (steep).
At the top (still) overcame the group as they (admire) the (amaze) beautiful
view. The (enjoy) experienced on that day (fill) them with (glad). The rest of
the students were (envy) and (hope) they would also have the opportunity
to go on the (out).

To add a suffix that begins with a vowel to a single syllable word that ends in a
single short vowel and a single consonant, double the final consonant and add
the suffix:

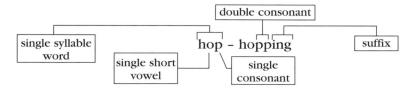

If the suffix begins with a consonant this rule does not apply:

glad – gladly

| single consonant | consonant |

Word list

bagful	joyful	spotty
fitting	manhood	stoppable
gladly	planned	strapped
gunned	rotting	wetness
hopped	sitting	wrapping
hugged	slipped	

Exercise 14

a. Copy and complete this table.

	+er	+est	+ness
wet	wetter	wettest	wetness
hot			
flat			
thin			
big			

b. Add the suffix -hood, -ment *or* -ed to these words. Remember the rules and spell the words correctly.

grin, boy, fit, pay, step

c. Add -er *and* -ly to these words. Remember the rules and spell the words correctly.

flat, hot, mad, sad

d. Write one sentence using any three words in the list on page 59.

To add a suffix to a multi-syllable word when the stress falls on the last syllable, double the final consonant and add the suffix:

refer – re • fer + ing = referring

suffix

two syllables   double consonant

Word list			
refer**r**ing	o**mit**ted	**gal**loping	**lim**ited
for**get**ting	re**gret**table	**car**peting	**ben**efited
for**got**ten	com**mit**ted	**com**fortable	**gar**dener
oc**cur**red	for**bid**den	**prof**itable	**al**teration
be**gin**ning	coun**cil**lor	**tar**geting	**mur**muring

Exercise 15

a. **Write the words in the list on page 60 in alphabetical order. Set them out like this:**

   alter + tion = alteration

b. **Use the rule to help you add the suffixes to these words.**

   for**get** + ing, for**bid** + ing, per**mit** + ing, quar**rel** + ed, com**pel** + ing, mar**vel** + ous

c. **Read these words aloud and try to decide which part of the word is stressed. Add the suffix -ed to each word.**

   Hint: The same part is stressed in each word.

   enter, order, limit, market, pardon

d. **Write a sentence using any three words in the word list on page 60.**

e. **Cover the word list on page 60 and test yourself to check that you can add these suffixes and spell the words correctly.**

   refer + ed = _____   gallop + ed = _____

   forgot + en = _____   begin + ing = _____

   carpet + ed = _____   regret + ed = _____

   forbid + ing = _____   garden + ing = _____

To add a suffix to a word ending in l:

◆ double the l if there is a single vowel before the l

◆ do not double the l if there is a double vowel before the l.

For example:

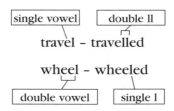

Word list

boil	label	quarrel	school
control	mail	rail	seal
fail	model	rebel	soil
fair	parcel	reveal	
foul	patrol	rival	
fulfil	propel	sail	

Exercise 16

a. **Apply the rules and add the suffix -ed to the words in the list.**

For example: rebel – rebelled.

b. **Choose the correct word in brackets and then write these sentences.**

As we (travelled / traveled) across the country we (marveled / marvelled) at the beautiful scenery.

The children (revealled/revealed) creative talent while (modelling/modeling) the clay.

He (cancelled / canceled) his (sailling / sailing) trip.

The shiny (metalic / metallic) car was (stealing / stealling) the limelight.

The students (rebelled / rebeled) against the high (faillure / failure) rate.

c. **Choose words from the word list above to complete these sentences.**

The police _____ed the area.

The _____ing clubs _____ed about the foul.

He _____ed the goalkeeper and was sent off the field.

She _____ed the parcel and _____ed it across the country.

In _____ness to the students, school should close when it is _____ing hot like this.

Do you remember?
The letter **y** counts as a vowel when added as a suffix.

To add a suffix beginning with a vowel to a word ending in a silent e, drop the silent e:

hope + ing = hoping

There are some exceptions to the rule. You usually keep the silent e when:

◆ the suffix begins with a consonant:

    engage + ment = engagement   polite + ly = politely

◆ the suffixes -able and -ous are added to words that contain a soft g or c:

    courage + ous = courageous

◆ the word may be mistaken for another word:

    dye + ing = dyeing (not dying)

◆ adding -age to the words line and mile.

To add a suffix to a word ending in -ie, drop the e and change the i to y:

    die – dying

(Look how odd *diing* looks. Can you understand why this is an exception to the rule?)

Word list

exciting	engagement	courageous	dyeing	lineage	dying
engaging	excitement	manageable		mileage	lying
hoping	immediately	noticeable			
replacing	replacement	outrageous			
survival	politely				

Exercise 17

a. **How does the meaning of *dying* differ from *dyeing*?**

b. **Match each set of words in the list to the appropriate rule.**

c. **Add -ing to these words.**

    face, invite, tie, note, provide, reduce, pollute, invite, smoke, increase

d. **Add -al to these words.**

    tribe, arrive, recite, tide, bride, approve, remove, refuse, universe, nature

e. **Write these sentences using the correct forms of the words in brackets.**

    We enjoyed (tie) and (dye) our t-shirts.

    It was (outrage) how many children were (lie).

    The disease is (cure).

    He damaged his (spine) column in the accident.

    The book was (surprise) good.

    Her accuracy when (calculate) is (note).

To add a suffix to a word that ends in -ic:

◆ add k before adding -ed, -er, -ing or -y:

  picnic + ed = picnic**k**ed

◆ add al before adding -ly:

  dramatic + ly = dramatic**al**ly

Word list

frolicking	trafficking	logically
mimicking	academically	medically
panicking	energetically	pathetically
picnicking		

Exercise 18

a. Write the words from the word list above like this:

  picnic + ing = picnicking

b. Add the suffix -ed to these words.

  picnic, traffic, mimic, frolic, panic

c. Add the suffix -ly to these words and then use the words in sentences that show you understand their meaning.

  clinic, comic, tragic, dynamic, dramatic

Do not double the final consonant when adding a suffix that begins with a vowel if:

◆ the word has more than one syllable *and*

◆ the final syllable has two vowels.

For example:

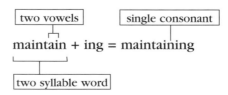

Word list

despair	complain	explain	abstain
entertain	avoid	honour	remain
appear	detain	repair	exploit

Exercise 19

a. **Write the words in the word list above in alphabetical order and underline the double vowel combination.**

b. **Add the suffixes -ed and -ing to the words from the word list above.**

For example: maintain – maintained – maintaining.

c. **Add the suffix -able to these words.**

favour, fashion, honour, repair, explain

d. **Apply the rules you have learnt to add the suffixes to these words.**

flavour + ed = _____, regret + ing = _____, travel + er = _____,

labour + ed = _____, music + ly = _____, picnic + ing = _____,

nation +al = _____, favour + able = _____, repel + ing = _____,

caution + ed = _____

e. **Rewrite this paragraph using the correct form of the words in brackets.**

I (despair) when my mother (comment) on my (appear) again. I have (explain) that it is (fashion), but she has not (abstain) from (comment). (Maintain) my stylish reputation is (become) more and more difficult.

Do you remember?

Revise the rules for adding affixes and then complete the following exercises.

Exercise 20

a. **Write the word that is spelt correctly in each pair.**

1. hopful / hopeful
2. beautifull / beautiful
3. relyable / reliable
4. heavyly / heavily
5. likeable / likable
6. emptyness / emptiness
7. arguement / argument

8. bagfull / bagful
9. sliped / slipped
10. refering / referring
11. forbiden / forbidden
12. benefitted / benefited
13. dieing / dying

14. couragous / courageous
15. panicing / panicking
16. comically / comicly
17. tryed / tried
18. lying / lieing
19. cureable / curable

b. Add prefixes to make these words mean the opposite.

possible, common, experienced, literate, respect

c. Copy and complete this table.

	+ ed	+ ing
convey	conveyed	conveying
rely		
deny		
hope		
obey		
pity		

d. Put the pieces together and write the correctly spelt word.

im + move + able = _____   ir + regular + ity = _____

dis + solve + able = _____   il + logic + al = _____

all + right = _____   pre + caution + ary = _____

dis + honest + ly = _____   dis + please + ed = _____

il + legal + ly = _____   un + employ + ment = _____

Word endings

It is easy to muddle the endings of some words because many of them sound similar. There are tips to help you choose the correct ending for some words, but some endings just have to be learnt.

1. Endings that sound the same or similar

Words ending in -ick and -ic

Many words end with the sound ic. For example:

kick   trick   mimic   panic

Use the rules to help you decide whether to spell the words with an ick or ic ending.

One syllable words end in -ick. For example: **sick**

Words with more than one syllable end in -ic. For example: traf • **fic**

Word list			
click	sick	chronic	panic
flick	stick	comic	strategic
kick	thick	ethnic	static
lick	trick	fantastic	traffic

Exercise 1

a. **Choose words from the word list above that mean the same as these words.**

   tactical, long-lasting, cultural, still

b. **Choose words from the word list above that mean the opposite of these words.**

   humourless, ordinary, calm, mobile

c. **Revise the suffix rule (see page 64) and then add -ly to these adjectives to change them to adverbs.**

   strategic, fantastic, comic, chronic

d. **Use a dictionary to help you write definitions for these words.**

   acoustic, authentic, aerobic, ceramic, eccentric

➤

e. Use the following words to complete the note below.

Nick, energetic, topic, tragic, fantastic, hectic, horrific, tonic, sick, scientific, magical, Arctic, traffic

Dear _____

We had a _____ time on our _____ exploration to the _____ Ocean. There were no crowds or _____ _____ in sight. We enjoyed researching the _____ and are very happy that there was not a _____ accident. It was _____ that Rick's mother died while he was away.

It was a pity that you were _____ and missed out on this _____ trip. Hopefully you will be able to join us next time. Start taking a _____ now so you are healthy and _____.

Regards

Eric

f. Write three sentences using as many of the words in the word list on page 67 as possible.

Words ending in -ible and -able

There are many more -able than -ible words so when in doubt and you do not have a dictionary nearby, choose -able.

Many of the -ible words are seldom heard so it is helpful to learn the most common -ible words and use -able for the rest.

Here are some tips that may help you decide which ending to use.

For words that end in **-able**, if you remove the ending you are usually left with a complete word:

presentable = present + able

Words with i before the ending usually end in -able:

sociable

The suffix -able is often used after a hard c or g:

applicable   navigable

For words that end in **-ible**, if you remove the ending you are usually not left with a complete word:

visible = vis + ible

Words with s or ss before the ending usually end in -ible:

sensible   possible

The suffix -ible is often used after a soft c or g:

legible   invincible

Word list

End in -able

reasonable	manageable
irritable	reliable
sociable	fashionable
comfortable	honourable

End in -ible

possible	horrible
edible	visible
terrible	resistible
sensible	flexible

Exercise 2

a. **Write the words in the word list above in alphabetical order.**

b. **How do the words 'irritable' and 'resistible' break the rules?**

c. **Which other words in the list break the rules?**

d. **Write the words from the list that are made up of a smaller word and a suffix. Underline the smaller word.**

For example: <u>reason</u>able.

e. **Many of the -ible words form opposites when you add the prefixes in-, il-, ir- and im-. Form the opposites of the following words.**

possible, edible, visible, resistible, flexible, legible

f. **Find words in the word list to match each of the following meanings.**

fit for eating, friendly, easily bent, can be seen, morally upright

g. **Cover the words in the list then copy and complete these words.**

soc _ _ _ _ _, poss _ _ _ _, rel _ _ _ _ _, vis _ _ _ _, hono _ _ _ _ _ _,
flex _ _ _ _, ed _ _ _ _, resis _ _ _ _ _, reas _ _ _ _ _ _, fash _ _ _ _ _ _ _

Words ending in -er, -or and -ar

The suffixes -er, -or and -ar sound very similar so it is difficult to know which one to choose. There are no rules to help you, but there are some tips on page 70.

The suffix -er is the one to choose if you are unsure as there are ten times more words ending in -er than -or and -ar put together.

The suffix -or is usually used when the word means 'that which' or 'someone who'. It is often used when the word ends in -ate, -ct or -it.

An actor is **someone who** acts: ac**t** + or = actor

An editor is **someone who** edits: edi**t** + or = editor

A calculator is **that which** calculates: calcul**ate** + or = calculator

Words that use -ar often finish in -lar:

scholar   solar

-er	-or	-ar
explorer	actor	altar
father	author	cellar
fighter	calculator	lunar
listener	doctor	popular
minister	editor	regular
mother	narrator	scholar
owner	spectator	similar
reporter	visitor	solar

Exercise 3

a. **Which -ar words in the table above are exceptions to the tips given?**

b. **Write down as many words ending in -lar as you can.**

c. **Write a word from the table to match each definition.**

   one who discovers new places   one who writes books

   one who corrects and prepares   one who tells stories
   texts for publication
                                          one who is learned

d. **Write words from the table that mean the same as these words.**

   preacher, alike, basement, onlooker, consistent

e. **Write the words from the table that have been made from these words.**

   own, visit, narrate, report, listen, fight

f. Cover the words in the table and correct these words.

lunor, regulor, fightor, celler, populer, ministar, fathor, editer, solor, auther

g. Apply the tips and find the word in each row that is correctly spelt.

operater	operator	operatar
collecter	collector	collectar
similer	similor	similar
musculer	musculor	muscular
spectaculer	spectaculor	spectacular
composer	composor	composar
stranger	strangor	strangar
celluler	cellulor	cellular
equater	equator	equatar
treasurer	treasuror	treasurar

Words ending in -ant, -ent, -ance and -ence

Words ending in -ant and -ent are usually adjectives. For example:

An ignor**ant** scholar.

| adjective |

Words ending in -ance and -ence are usually nouns. For example:

The ignor**ance** of the scholar.

| noun |

The suffix -ance often appears after the letter t or v. For example:

impor**t**ance relevance

Word list			
difference	continent	elegance	competent
different	conference	elegant	competence
important	frequent	urgent	relevance
importance	radiance	confidence	advance
significant	radiant	brilliance	acceptance
significance	reference	brilliant	assistance

71

Exercise 4

a. Write the words in the word list on page 71 in alphabetical order in a table like this.

-ant	-ance	-ent	-ence
brilliant	acceptance	competent	competence
elegant			

b. Write five sentences, each of which should include an adjective from the list.

c. Change the following adjectives to nouns by changing their endings.

   different, important, confident, radiant, intelligent

d. Change the following nouns to adjectives by changing their endings.

   importance, significance, elegance, magnificence, persistence

e. Add the prefix in- or un- to form the opposite of each of these words.

   different, important, significant, frequent, confident

f. Write a sentence using each pair of words given.

   importance, continent

   radiance, elegant

   competent, brilliance

Words ending in -ary and -ery

The suffixes -ary and -ery cause confusion because they sound the same:

   stationery   stationary

If in doubt, choose -ary as it is a more common ending.

The e in -ery is sometimes not pronounced:

   cemetery

Do you remember?

Synonyms are words with similar meanings, for example: hot and boiling.

Word list

stationary	literary	primary	surgery
stationery	tertiary	jewellery	imaginary
cemetery	slavery	temporary	necessary
secondary	February	bribery	bravery
library	boundary	delivery	nursery
discovery	query	dictionary	elementary

Exercise 5

a. **Write the words from the word list above in alphabetical order in a table like this.**

-ary	-ery
bound<u>ary</u>	brav<u>e</u>ry

b. **Highlight the e and a letters in the words in your table that you don't necessarily sound out when you say the word.**

c. **Look up these words in the dictionary and write them in order from first to last.**

tertiary, primary, elementary, secondary

d. **Write a word from the word list above to match each definition.**

a request for information

a place where books are kept

a place where plants are grown

not lasting for long

something that is essential

e. **Write words from the word list that are associated with these words.**

finding, paper, graveyard, fictional, immobile, courage, operation, border

➢

f. Copy these sentences and complete them with words from the word list on page 73.

When _____ was abolished people were given their freedom.

I received a special _____ on my birthday.

The author received a special _____ award.

_____ is the shortest month.

It is against the law to be involved in _____ and corruption.

g. What is the root word of the following?

jewellery, dictionary

Do you remember?

Antonyms are words that mean the opposite, for example: hot and cold.

Words ending in -acle, -cal and -icle

Most words that end in -cal are adjectives and most words that end in -acle or -icle are nouns.

Word list
Read and learn how to spell these words.

practical	identical	topical	particle
vehicle	spectacle	miracle	vertical
obstacle	tentacle	icicle	logical
article	physical	oracle	focal

Exercise 6

a. Sort the words in the word list above into the following three groups.

-acle nouns	-cal adjectives	-icle nouns

b. Look up the following words in the dictionary and write their definitions.

tentacle, icicle, oracle, particle, vertical

➤

c. **Write words from the word list on page 74 that mean the opposite of the following.**

impractical, different

d. **Write a sentence using each pair of words.**

   1. practical, vehicle

   2. identical, icicle

   3. topical, miracle

e. **Divide these words into syllables.**

physical, practical, identical

f. **Write the sentences using the correct form of the word in brackets.**

It was a (miraculous) that he did not break his neck in the diving accident.

On New Year's Eve we watched a (spectacular) of fireworks.

g. **Find a word in the word list on page 74 to fit in with each group of words.**

   1. motorbike, car, truck

   2. twins, triplets, quadruplets

   3. prophet, prophetess, priest

   4. upright, erect, perpendicular

   5. show, display, sight

Words ending in -cede, -ceed and -sede

The only word in English that ends in -sede is supersede.

Exceed, proceed and succeed are the only words ending in -ceed.

All the other words ending with this sound end in -cede.

Word list		
supersede	exceed	accede
	proceed	cede
	succeed	concede
		intercede
		precede
		recede

Exercise 7

a. Use a dictionary to help you match each word in the word list on page 75 to one of these definitions.

go back or down

happen before something

go beyond expected limits

agree with something

begin doing something

achieve what was planned

unwillingly admit something

surrender or give up something

take the place or position of something or someone

settle a disagreement between other people

b. Write antonyms from the word list on page 75 for these words.

follow, deny, fail, reject

c. Find the word in each pair that is spelt correctly.

1. preceed	precede	**6.** recede	receed	
2. proceed	procede	**7.** ceed	cede	
3. intersede	intercede	**8.** concede	conceed	
4. succeed	suceed	**9.** supersede	supercede	
5. secede	seceed	**10.** exceed	excede	

d. Copy and complete these words without referring back to the word list on page 75.

con_____, ac_____, super_____, re_____, inter_____,
ex_____, pro_____, suc_____, pre_____, c_____

Words ending in -le, -el and -al

There are many words that end in -le.

The -el ending is far less common so it is best to learn the words that are spelt with -el.

The suffix -al is added to adjectives and nouns to talk about things that are linked to the root word. For example: comical means things that are funny, annual means each year.

If you are unsure of the ending of a word, try spelling it different ways. Then ask yourself which way looks right.

Word list			
rural	riddle	eagle	chuckle
idle	hostel	sample	scalpel
panel	local	snorkel	kennel
jewel	model	rebel	title
label	parcel	example	personal
ample	novel	survival	national
principal	signal	professional	cancel

Exercise 8

a. **Sort the words in the word list above into three lists according to how they end.**

b. **Copy these words and add the correct ending.**

chuck_____, snork_____, nation_____, canc_____,
samp_____, surviv_____, id_____, lab_____, profession_____,
host_____, amp_____

c. **Add the suffix -ed to these words.**

idle, label, sample, rebel, chuckle, cancel, knife

d. **Write synonyms from the word list above for these words.**

lazy, resident, name, sign, puzzle, board

➤

77

e. Is each sentence true or false? Correct the false sentences using words from the word list on page 77.

An eagle can be a bird or a golf score.

Farms are usually found in urban areas.

An example shows you how to do something.

A rebel protests against something.

Private relates to public affairs.

f. Choose the word in each row that looks correct. Check in your dictionary to see if you made the correct choices.

1. normle   normel   normal

2. settle   settel   settal

3. equle   equel   equal

4. generle   generel   general

5. invisible   invisibel   invisibal

6. possible   possibel   possibal

7. camle   camel   camal

8. travle   travel   traval

Words ending in -tion and -sion

If a word ending sounds like shun, it is probably spelt -tion.

If a word ending sounds a bit like zhin, it is probably spelt -sion.

To add -tion or -sion to a word you need to change the word a little.

Word list			
decorate	decoration	locate	location
collide	collision	revise	revision
observe	observation	navigate	navigation
confuse	confusion	televise	television
quote	quotation	refrigerate	refrigeration
decide	decision	conclude	conclusion
erode	erosion		

Exercise 9

a. Look at the word list on page 78 and find the patterns used to add -tion and -sion.

b. Use the patterns to help you add -sion to these words. Check your spelling using a dictionary.

explode, fuse, exclude, include, erode

c. Sort the words in the word list on page 78 into verbs and nouns.

d. Write a word ending in -tion or -sion to match each clue.

a specific place

you catch a train here

paying attention to something

TV

your sight, beginning with v

a warning beginning with c

direction finding

cooling system

e. Copy and complete the sentences using words from the word list on page 78.

We will decorate the tree with green and red _____.

After studying the problem for hours, I have come to the _____ it cannot be solved.

Luckily no one was hurt in the _____, but it caused a traffic jam.

You need to _____ your spelling rules before the test.

At the sound of the fire alarm _____ broke out as everyone fled in different directions.

I cannot _____ whether I should study or watch _____.

The _____ for the building alterations was very high.

You must plant trees to help prevent soil _____.

Words ending in -eer, -ere and -ier

Do you remember?
Homophones are words that sound the same, but have different spellings and meanings.

To help you to remember how to spell a word, try to find smaller words within it. For example:

revere   in**since**re

Word list	jeer	insincere	volunteer
cheer			
engineer	interfere	frontier	angrier
severe	pier	adhere	amplifier
sincere	hemisphere	tier	carrier
persevere	barrier	sneer	peer
	revere	cashier	veer

a. **Write the words from the word list above in three lists according to their ending. List them in alphabetical order and then highlight the shorter words found within the words. Not all the words have shorter words within them.**

b. **Copy and complete these words.**

volunt _ _ _, hemisph _ _ _, persev _ _ _, barr _ _ _, int _ _ _ ere, amp _ _ _ ier, si _ _ ere, e _ _ _ neer

c. **Write the two words in the word list above that are homophones. Use them in sentences that explain their meaning.**

d. **Match a word in the word list above to each definition.**

a border between countries

to change direction suddenly

very harsh

to obey or follow someone or something

to not be genuine or show one's true feelings

to admire and respect someone

e. **Name these people who end in -eer. Use the words below to help you.**

   puppeteer, auctioneer, mountaineer, pioneer, overseer, volunteer

   a person who works for no money

   a person who is in charge of an auction

   a person who is the first to do something

   a person who operates puppets

   a person who climbs mountains

   a person who supervises

f. **Find synonyms in the word list on page 80 to match these words.**

   teller, level, job, madder, scoff, transporter

Words ending in -ought, -aught and -ough

Not many words end in -ought and even fewer end in -aught. You probably only use two words ending in -aught. Can you think what these are?

The ending -ough has different sounds. For example:

   the oh sound in dough   the ow sound in plough

   the oo sound in through   the uff sound in enough.

Word list			
tough	distraught	taught	although
ought	brought	through	onslaught
caught	fought	dough	enough
rough	sought	plough	fraught
bought	nought	thought	drought

Exercise 11

a. Sort the words in the word list on page 81 into a table similar to this one.

-ought	-aught	-ough sounds like oh	-ough sounds like oo	-ough sounds like ow	-ough sounds like uff

b. Use a dictionary to help you write definitions for these words.

onslaught, distraught, plough, sought

c. Write a sentence using each set of words.

1. taught, caught, rough

2. fought, tough, although

3. thought, nought, enough

4. ought, bought, brought

d. Write the sentences that show the correct meaning of the underlined word.

The rope was <u>taught</u> so I struggled to loosen it.

My teacher <u>taught</u> me how to spell supercalifragilisticexpialidocious.

I slithered <u>through</u> the dark narrow tunnel.

I <u>through</u> the ball as far as I could.

The beautiful <u>dough</u> looked at me then ran into the forest to join the buck.

I kneaded the <u>dough</u> to make bread.

e. Use the word list above to help you complete these words.

b _ _ ght, s _ _ ght, th _ _ ght, r _ _ gh, en _ _ _ _, n _ _ ght, t _ _ ght,
c _ _ ght, distr _ _ _ _ _, onsl _ _ _ _ _, thr _ _ _ _, d _ _ gh, pl _ _ gh,
br _ _ ght, f _ _ ght, alth _ _ _ _

2. More word endings

Words ending in -ous

The suffix **-ous** means:

◆ abounding in

◆ full of

◆ possessing the qualities of

◆ having or taking.

For example: piteous means full of pity.

Many adjectives end in the suffix -ous.

Saying the word out loud will help you decide if it should be spelt -ous, -ious or -eous.

Word list			
famous	enormous	cautious	courageous
serious	obvious	precious	humorous
jealous	anxious	generous	luxurious
gorgeous	previous	monstrous	pious
delicious	gracious	piteous	perilous

Exercise 12

a. **Write the words in the word list above in three different groups according to their endings. Write them in alphabetical order.**

b. **Copy these sentences and complete them with words from the word list.**

The poor hungry puppy had a _____ whine.

The _____ man risked his life to rescue the child.

The _____ movie star lived in a _____ mansion.

We found the comedian very _____.

It was _____ that the _____ girl would win the beauty contest.

c. **Write synonyms from the word list above for these words.**

sincere, envious, worried, careful, big

d. **Write antonyms from the word list above for these words.**

stingy, succeeding, ungracious, worthless, careless

➤

e. Use the word **monstrous** in a descriptive sentence.

f. Use the word list on page 83 to help you complete these words.

pit _ _ _ s, fam _ _ s, monstr _ _ s, ser _ _ _ s, gener _ _ s, jeal _ _ s,
gorg _ _ _ s, humor _ _ s, delic _ _ _ s, luxur _ _ _ s, enorm _ _ s, obv _ _ _ s,
courag _ _ _ s, anx _ _ _ s, prev _ _ _ s, grac _ _ _ s, caut _ _ _ s, prec _ _ _ s

Words ending in -ile

To change adjectives ending in the suffix -ile to nouns:

◆ drop the final e

◆ add -ity.

Word list

agile	fragile	pile	tile
compile	futile	profile	versatile
crocodile	meanwhile	reptile	volatile
fertile	missile	smile	vile
file	mobile	textile	worthwhile

Exercise 13

a. **Find two compound words in the word list above and use them in sentences that explain their meaning.**

b. **Copy these sentences and complete them with words from the word list above.**

He made a _____ attempt to catch his _____ phone before it fell into the water.

If you _____ a _____ of all your important notes you will find it easier to study.

A _____ and a lizard are scaly _____.

c. **Match each clue to a word in the word list above.**

not very strong   revolting

easily influenced   moving easily

this lights up the face

d. **Change the following adjectives to nouns.**

For example: versatile – versatility.

agile, futile, volatile, fragile, mobile

e. **Copy and complete this table. Ignore the shaded blocks.**

Word	Plural	Past tense	+ ing
file	files	filed	filing
tile			
smile			
compile			
textile			
missile			

f. **Use the word list on page 84 to help you complete these words.**

s _ _ le, vo _ _ _ ile, a _ _ le, co _ _ ile, m _ _ ile, me _ _ _ _ ile, ver _ _ _ ile,
wor _ _ _ hile, re _ _ ile, fr _ _ ile, mi _ _ ile, fu _ ile, cro _ _ _ ile, te _ _ ile

Words ending in -ment

Nouns can be formed by adding the suffix -ment to many verbs. For example:

manage – management.

Word list

cement	document	argument	experiment
enjoyment	element	attachment	improvement
segment	management	commitment	instrument
disappointment	fragment	compliment	environment
comment	statement	requirement	payment

Exercise 14

a. **Write the words in the word list above in alphabetical order and underline the small words found within words. Note: 'men' will appear in all words so only underline it if no other small words can be found.**

For example: arg<u>um</u>ent.

b. **Use a dictionary to help you write definitions for the first five words in your alphabetical list.** ➤

c. Write synonyms from the word list on page 85 for the following words.

piece, needed, better, praise, fun

d. Copy these sentences and complete them with words from the word list on page 85.

Please read the important _____ from the _____ of the company.

A tiny _____ of the china cup chipped off when I knocked it against the sink.

The _____ in my kettle is broken so I have to boil water on the stove.

The bank sent me a _____ which showed how much money was in the account.

We used the _____ to perform a science _____.

e. Write the following sentences using the correct form of the words in brackets.

The winning team experienced great (excite), but the losing team moaned with (disappoint).

There has been a huge (improve) in your marks this term.

Your (commit) to (improve) has been admirable.

The (argue) lead to a break in the (agree).

The (enjoy) experienced by the students on camp was talked about for days.

f. Use the word list on page 85 to help you complete these words.

c _ _ _ nt, man _ _ _ ment, en _ _ _ ment, s _ _ ment, st _ _ _ ment,
f _ _ _ ment, disap _ _ _ _ _ ment, com _ _ _ ment, com _ _ _ t,
imp _ _ _ _ ment, do _ _ _ ent, requ _ _ _ ment, e _ _ _ ent, ar _ _ _ ent,
at _ _ _ hment, comp _ _ _ _ nt, in _ _ _ _ _ ent, expe _ _ _ ent

Words ending in -ue

The sound made by the ending -ue is also made by the following letter combinations:

food   few   fruit   through

Word list

argue	construe	issue	statue
avenue	cue	pursue	tissue
blue	due	queue	true
clue	flue	rescue	value
continue	glue	subdue	venue

Exercise 15

a. Match these clues to words in the word list above.

to be correct

a detective looks at these

a sticky substance

to save someone

to quieten down

use when you have a cold

b. Find words in the word list above to complete these sentences.

I _____ his silence to mean that he is happy for us to go.

_____ walking along the _____ until you see a stone _____ in front of a park.

The _____ is ideal for a music concert.

I hope we do not have to stand in a long _____ for tickets.

I will _____ a career in marketing.

c. Write synonyms for these words.

line, keep going, follow, place

d. Write homophones from the word list above to match these words.

blew, dew

e. Now use the words in sentences that show their different meanings.

For example: too – two.

There were <u>too</u> many entries so I knew I didn't have a good chance of winning one of the <u>two</u> prizes.

➤

87

f. Write sentences that show these words being used in two different ways. You may need to refer to your dictionary to find different meanings.

cue, issue, value, blue, pursue

g. Use the word list on page 87 to help you complete these words.

d _ _, ti _ _ ue, cons _ _ _ _, b _ _ e, gl _ _, ve _ ue, va _ ue, q _ _ _ e, av _ _ ue, re _ _ ue, st _ _ ue, c _ _, t _ _ e, pu _ _ ue, su _ _ ue, con _ _ _ ue, cl _ _, i _ _ ue

Words ending in -ise

Many words ending in the suffix -ise are verbs.

Most words ending in -ise are spelt with an s in British English. You may see them spelt with -ize at the end in American English.

Word list

exercise	civilise	familiarise	summarise
accessorise	colonise	idolise	organise
advertise	criticise	visualise	apologise
agonise	devise	supervise	televise
baptise	energise	emphasise	victimise

Exercise 16

a. Write the words in the word list above in alphabetical order and then divide them into syllables. Pronounce each syllable.

For example: exercise – ex • er • cise.

b. Change each of these words into a noun. Say 'the', 'a' or 'an' before the noun to check that you have made the correct choice.

For example: advertise – (an) advertisement.

accessorise, baptise, civilise, colonise, idolise, emphasise

➤

c. **Match a word from the word list on page 88 to each meaning.**

to say sorry

to stress something

to oversee an activity

to critique something

to promote something

to imagine something

to do physical activities

to plan something

to bring order

d. **Write words from the word list on page 88 that were made from these words.**

energy, agony, summary, familiar, visual, apology

e. **Use the word list on page 88 to help you complete these words.**

dev _ _ _, e _ _ _ cise, en _ _ gise, a _ _ e _ _ orise, ad _ _ _ _ ise, c _ _ _ nise,
b _ _ tise, em _ _ asise, ci _ _ _ ise, cri _ _ _ ise, su _ _ arise, fami _ _ _ _ ise,
id _ _ ise, vis _ _ lise, sup _ _ vise, org _ _ ise, apo _ _ gise, agon _ _ _

Words ending in -ive

Listen for the two different ways in which the suffix -ive is pronounced:

al**ive**   crea**tive**

Word list			
alive	captive	contrive	strive
active	adjective	constructive	thrive
creative	massive	jive	competitive
survive	connive	attractive	passive
forgive	expensive	positive	sensitive
arrive	digestive	destructive	negative

Exercise 17

a. **Divide the words in the word list above into two columns according to how the suffix is pronounced.**

b. Copy and complete these sentences.

The _____ artist bought _____ oil paints.

To _____ in the desert you had better _____ to make your water last.

The _____ hoped to _____ an escape plan.

The _____ quote won the company a _____ contract.

The _____ toddler will _____ and keep us running all day.

c. Write three pairs of antonyms that appear in the word list on page 89. Use the antonyms in sentences that show you understand the meanings of the words.

d. Copy and complete these common expressions with words from the word list on page 89.

_____ and forget   Dead or _____

e. Match a word in the word list on page 89 to each meaning.

a descriptive word

easily offended and annoyed

a lively dance

do or grow well

a system that helps us break down food

good-looking

f. Change these words so they end in the suffix -ity.

For example: active – activity.

creative, captive, positive, passive, sensitive, negative

g. Use the word list on page 89 to help you complete these words.

a _ _ ec _ ive, ma _ _ ive, des _ _ _ _ tive, comp _ _ _ tive, str _ _ _, th _ _ ve, co _ _ ive, a _ ive, a _ tive, cr _ _ tive, s _ _ vive, f _ _ give, ar _ _ ve, ca _ _ ive, cons _ _ _ _ tive, j _ _ _, at _ _ _ _ tive, po _ _ _ ive, pa _ _ ive, sen _ _ _ ive, ne _ _ tive, ex _ _ _ sive, _ _ gestive, con _ _ ive

Words ending in -ct

You can add the suffix -ion to many words ending in -ct to form nouns. For example:

construct – construction.

Word list

act	subtract	obstruct	extract
tact	product	abstract	architect
pact	predict	collect	deduct
conflict	affect	contract	instinct
construct	attract	defect	neglect
addict	impact	extinct	instruct

Exercise 18

a. **Write the words in the word list above in alphabetical order and then divide them into syllables. Pronounce each syllable.**

b. **Change each of these words into a noun.**

addict, attract, construct, extract

c. **Write sentences that show the words below being used in two different ways. You may need to refer to your dictionary to find different meanings.**

For example:

Practise reading an **extract** of the story aloud.

The dentist is going to **extract** four of my teeth.

extract, act, conflict, product, collect, contract

d. **Match the synonyms.**

diplomacy	attract
hinder	construct
agreement	tact
entice	predict
teach	collect
forecast	obstruct
build	instruct
fetch	pact

e. Write antonyms from the word list on page 91 for these words.

add, flawless, care, living, practical

f. Copy and complete the sentences below.

If you subtract the product of 2 and 12 from 100, the answer is _____.

If you deduct 10 from the product of 7 and 8 the answer is _____.

If you become a television _____ it will _____ on your life in a negative way and _____ your friendships.

The _____ relies on knowledge and _____ when designing buildings.

g. Use the word list on page 91 to help you complete these words.

ne _ _ ect, a _ _, in _ _ _ uct, t _ _ _, de _ _ ct, in _ _ inct, p _ _ _, a _ _ _ itect, con _ _ ict, e _ tr _ ct, c _ _ struct, a _ _ ict, sub _ _ _ _ t, e _ tin _ t, pr _ _ uct, cont _ _ _ _, pr _ _ ict, af _ _ _ t, _ _ fect, a _ _ ract, im _ _ _ _, obs _ _ _ _ _, abs _ _ act, co _ _ ect

Words ending in -ual

You can change adjectives ending in -ual to adverbs by adding -ly. For example:

equal – equally.

Word list			
dual	factual	manual	perpetual
equal	actual	virtual	spiritual
casual	gradual	contextual	individual
visual	punctual	intellectual	
annual	mutual	unusual	

Exercise 19

a. Write the words in the word list above in alphabetical order and identify and underline the parts of the words that you find tricky.

➢

b. Copy and complete these sentences.

Look at the _____ clues to work out the meanings of words.

You do not have to be highly _____ to achieve good marks.

We have a _____ agreement to respect one another.

A _____ leader from America spoke at our church.

I have never seen anything as _____ as that statue.

It is important to be _____ for the meeting.

The _____ budget is printed in a _____ and discussed at the _____ meeting.

c. Use your dictionary to help you write definitions for these words.

virtual, perpetual, dual

d. Match each word to its synonym.

casual	slow
equal	separate
factual	informal
gradual	optical
individual	identical
visual	accurate

e. Change these adjectives to adverbs.

unusual, perpetual, spiritual, annual, visual, gradual

f. Use the word list on page 92 to help you complete these words.

act _ _ _, an _ _ al, c _ su _ l, con _ _ _ tual, d _ _ l, e _ ual, fa _ _ ual,
g _ _ _ ual, indi _ _ _ ual, in _ _ _ _ ectual, ma _ _ al, mu _ _ al, per _ _ _ ual,
pun _ _ ual, _ _ _ ritual, _ _ usual, v _ _ tual, vi _ ual

Words ending in -us

You can form plurals by adding es to most words ending in -us.

With some words you have the option to drop the -us and add i. For example:

cactus – cactuses or cacti.

Word list

focus	campus	cactus	asparagus
circus	minus	eucalyptus	platypus
chorus	status	consensus	fungus
discus	census	walrus	apparatus
virus	surplus	octopus	abacus

Exercise 20

a. **Write the words in the word list above in alphabetical order and say them out loud, over-exaggerating the pronunciation.**

b. **In the word list above find:**

   three animals   four plants.

c. **Write the plural form of these words.**

   chorus, circus, discus, octopus, status, virus

d. **Brainstorm as many synonyms as you can for these words.**

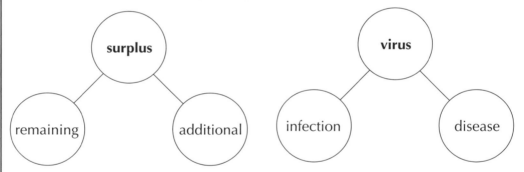

e. **Write this sentence and correct the spellings of the words in brackets.**

   The (focis) on (cumpus) this term has been to get a (concensus) about whether or not the (platipus) should appear (minis) its bill.

f. **Use the word list above to help you complete these words.**

   as _ _ _ agus, c _ _ tus, c _ _ pus, c _ _ sus, c _ _ rus, c _ _ cus, con _ _ _ sus,
   di _ _ us, euca _ _ _ tus, fo _ us, _ _ _ gus, m _ nus, oc _ _ pus, pla _ _ pus,
   st _ _ us, sur _ _ us, vi _ us, w _ _ rus

Sneaky letters

In English, some words have letters in them that are very hard to hear or even silent. This makes it difficult to sound out the words and to apply spelling rules. For most of the words in this chapter, it is best to learn to spell them using whichever method you find easiest.

1. Silent letters

Some words have silent letters that you cannot hear when you say the word, but which you obviously have to include when you write the word.

Silent e

The silent e is the most common silent letter in English. You have already learnt how the silent e at the end of a word can change the vowel sounds in the word (see page 14). You also know how to add suffixes to words that end with a silent e. Read through this summary of the rules to revise them.

An e at the end of a word that ends with a vowel followed by a consonant gives the word a long vowel sound. This means you pronounce the vowel as ay, ee, eye, oh or you. For example:

   a: cake   e: these   i: pipe   o: smoke   u: fuse

To add a suffix that starts with a consonant, keep the silent e at the end of the root word and add the suffix. For example:

   hope + ful = hopeful   complete + ly = completely   care + less = careless

To add a suffix that starts with a vowel or a y, drop the silent e at the end of the root word and add the suffix. For example:

   change + ed = changed   value + able = valuable
   nerve + ous = nervous   use + age = usage

Exercise 1

These words are all spelt incorrectly. Apply the rules and write the correct spelling of each word.

accuratly, achievment, advertisment, argueing, arrangment, befor, completly, diffrent, divineity, duely, forcful, hopful, intrested, judgeing, politness, tastless, truely, useage

---

Other silent letters

There are some exceptions to the rules below.

Letter that is silent	Examples
a	bread, deaf, meant, read, tread, board, parliament
b (after m or before t)	bomb, climb, comb, crumb, lamb, plumber, thumb debt, doubt, subtle
c (silent in sc)	muscle, scene, scenic, scent, science, scissors
d (always silent in dg)	bridge, edge, ledge, judge handkerchief, sandwich
g (always silent in gm and gn, not heard in ght sounds, the g is sometimes sounded in gnu)	paradigm, design, foreign, gnu, gnome, reign, sign bright, right, light, sight, caught, fright
h (silent at the beginning of words, in gh and after r or h)	heir, hour, honour, honest exhaust, exhibit rhythm, rhyme, rhino, rhombus shepherd, school ghetto, ghost, ghoul what, where, which, whip, whisper, whisk
i	bruise, business, medicine
k (silent in kn)	knee, knew, knife, knight, knit, knob, knot, know, knowledge, knuckle
l (silent after a, o, u)	calm, chalk, half, salmon, should, talk, would, yolk
m	mnemonic
n (silent in mn at the end of words)	autumn, column, government, hymn, solemn
p (silent in pn, ps and pt)	pneumatic, psalm, psychology, pterodactyl, receipt
s	aisle, island, isle
t (silent after s, hard to hear in words ending in -tch)	castle, listen, mortgage, rustle, whistle watch, fetch, itch
u	biscuit, build, guess, guest, guitar, plague
w (silent before r, may not be heard in words starting with wh)	wreck, wrist, write, wrong, wrote who, whole, whose
x, y and z (words from other languages)	grand prix eye rendezvous

Exercise 2

a. Find all the silent letters in these words.

tomb, board, aisle, subtle, Tuesday, hymn, whole, height, solemn, condemn, psychologist, answer, vague, guest, thistle

b. There are silent letters missing from these words. Copy the words and fill in the missing letters to spell them correctly.

_onesty, dou_t, thum_, num_, _our, _nuckle, _nowle_ge, _rong, _nives, _neel, hym_, sc_olar, s_ord, clim_er, _rist, mus_le, _seudonym, We_nesday, ras_berry

2. Double consonants

Many words have double consonants. It can make a big difference in meaning if you use a single consonant in place of a double one. For example:

A **diner** eats her **dinner**.   A **dinner** eats her **diner**.

A dinner is a meal.

A diner is person who is eating a meal or a restaurant that serves meals.

Some words have double consonants because affixes have been added to them. For example:

ir + regular = irregular

usual + ly = usually

Double c – cc

Word list
Read and learn how to spell these words.

accelerate	accordion	cappuccinos	occupy
accent	account	desiccated	occur
accept	accountant	eccentric	preoccupied
access	accumulate	hiccup	raccoon
accident	accurate	moccasin	soccer
acclaim	accuse	occasion	success
accommodation	accustomed	occasionally	succumb
accomplish	broccoli	occupation	vaccination

Exercise 3

a. Divide the words in the word list on page 97 into syllables. Pronounce each syllable.

b. Match the words and definitions.

hiccup	a flat leather shoe
cappuccino	to go increasingly quickly
moccasin	to give in to something
accelerate	a person who works with financial records
succumb	a gulping sound
broccoli	to praise someone highly
accent	a way of pronouncing words
accountant	a musical instrument
acclaim	milky coffee with froth
accordion	a vegetable

c. Match the synonyms.

desiccated	crash
eccentric	receive
accident	entry
accomplish	dried
accept	unusual
accumulate	achieve
access	familiar
occasionally	happen
accustomed	sometimes
occur	gather

d. Use these words to complete the sentences.

vaccination, soccer, accommodation, accurate, accuse, occasion, occupation, occupy, success, account

We are looking for _____ to _____ for the entire summer holiday.

They need an _____ goal scorer in their _____ team if they want to achieve more _____.

She took the baby to the clinic to get her _____.

Do you have an _____ at a bank?

Do not _____ me of cheating.

We are celebrating a special _____.

I hope I have an interesting _____ when I grow up.

e. **Use ten of the words from the word list on page 97 in sentences that show you understand their meaning.**

Double f – ff

Word list
Read and learn how to spell these words.

affable	buffalo	graffiti	ruffle
affair	coffee	off	scaffold
affect	different	offence	scoffed
affectionate	difficult	offering	suffering
affix	effect	officer	sufficient
afford	efficient	offices	traffic
baffle	giraffe	official	whiff

Exercise 4

a. **Match the synonyms below and at the top of the next page.**

whiff   unsettle

ruffle   well-organised

offering   hard

efficient   smell

difficult   demonstrative

affectionate   pleasant

affable   attach

➤

affix	contribution
baffle	matter
affair	confuse

b. Use a dictionary to help you write definitions for these words.

offence, official, scaffold, graffiti, sufficient

c. Choose the correct form of each word in brackets and write the sentences.

The (effect, affect) of the robbery (effected, affected) us for ages.

Get (of, off) the table and sit on your chair.

The dealers were (trafficing, trafficking) goods illegally.

My father works in an (office, offices) that overlooks the sea.

I like the new girl as she is very (affable, affible).

d. Copy and complete this paragraph with suitable ff words.

I was standing on the _ _ _ ff _ _ _ drawing _ _ _ ff _ _ _ on the wall when an _ ff _ _ _ _ of the law stopped and told me I was committing a criminal _ ff _ _ _ _. He gave me an _ ff _ _ _ _ _ warning. I was thankful as I could not have _ ff _ _ _ _ to pay a fine. I was _ uff _ _ _ _ _ _ly embarrassed by the whole _ ff _ _ _. Next time I am bored I will make sure I do something _ _ ff _ _ _ _ _. Perhaps I should stay at home and drink _ _ ff _ _. My friends _ _ _ ff _ _ at my stupidity.

e. Write a sentence using each set of words.

giraffe, buffalo, suffering

baffle, whiff, coffee

scaffold, traffic, off

Double l – ll

> **Word list**
> Read and learn how to spell these words.
>
> | | | | |
> |---|---|---|---|
> | shallow | jewellery | parallel | allow |
> | valley | gallery | gallop | swallow |
> | collect | dull | intelligent | umbrella |
> | villain | college | bullet | recollect |
> | occasionally | millennium | gorilla | usually |
> | recall | accidentally | challenge | seagull |
> | caterpillar | fulfilled | village | allergic |
> | propeller | skill | marvellous | brilliant |

Exercise 5

a. **Which words in the word list above have double letters because a suffix has been added? Write them in alphabetical order.**

b. **Copy and complete this table.**

	+ ed	+ ing
allow	allowed	allowing
challenge		
gallop		
recall		
recollect		
swallow		

c. **Match the words below and on the next page to the definitions.**

accidentally	you see this flying over the sea looking for fish
bullet	this turns into a moth
gorilla	an evil character
millennium	you need this in the rain
seagull	not on purpose
caterpillar	a place to study
umbrella	a large ape
villain	a low-lying area between mountains

➤

college   1000 years

valley   ammunition used in a gun

d. Find antonyms in the word list on page 101 for these words.

bright, deep, stupid, forget, often

e. Copy and complete these sentences using words from the word list on page 101.

I went to the art _____ to see the exhibition.

The lines in a parallelogram run _____.

I would prefer living in a small _____ compared to a big city.

Can you _____ whether or not you have met her before?

My mother does not _____ me to _____ bubble gum.

Double m – mm

Word list
Read and learn how to spell these words.

accommodate	common	immense	shimmer
command	gimmick	immune	summary
commence	grammar	mammal	summer
comment	hammock	mammoth	summit
commit	immature	programme	summon
committee	immediate	recommend	swimming

Exercise 6

a. Use a dictionary to help you write definitions for these words:

gimmick, mammal, summit, committee, hammock

b. Match the synonyms.

immature   vast

accommodate   order

immense   call

command   gleam

shimmer	resistant
commence	childish
summon	start
immune	house
immediate	huge
mammoth	instantaneous

c. Copy and complete the sentences using these words:

summary, common, summit, comment, grammar, summer, commit, programme, hammock, recommend, swimming

I _____ that you _____ yourself to following a _____ _____ this _____ in order to get fit.

It is _____ to make a _____ of your notes when learning for a _____ test.

My negative _____ was criticised.

After many days of hiking they reached the _____ of the mountain.

I am going to lie in the _____ and read my book.

d. Write sentences that show two different meanings for each word:

summon, summit, gimmick, common, programme

Double n – nn

Word list

Read and learn how to spell these words.

announce	cannibal	cunning	pennant
annoying	cannot	dinner	questionnaire
antenna	centennial	funnel	sonnet
banner	channel	innocent	tunnel
beginning	cinnamon	mannequin	tyranny
bunny	connect	meanness	unnecessary

Exercise 7

a. **Write the words from the word list on page 103 and highlight any shorter words that appear within them.**

b. **Match the words to their definitions:**

antenna	a life-size dummy on which clothes are displayed
cannibal	a small triangular flag on ships so they can be identified
cinnamon	relating to a hundred years
channel	cruel use of power over people
centennial	a spice from the bark of a tree
tunnel	thin sensory organs found in pairs on some heads
mannequin	a strip of water between land
pennant	someone who eats people
sonnet	a passage through something
tyranny	a poem with 14 lines and a set structure

c. **List the four adjectives in the word list on page 103 that could replace the line in this sentence:**

My _____ little sister shares my room.

d. **Match the antonyms:**

beginning	necessary
connect	guilty
cannot	ending
innocent	kindness
meanness	disconnect
unnecessary	can

e. **Write sentences using these words:**

announce, funnel, dinner, questionnaire, bunny

Double r – rr

Word list
Read and learn how to spell these words.

arrangement	conferring	narrow	sorry
array	correspond	occurring	strawberry
arrest	current	occurrence	surrender
barrel	embarrassed	parrot	surround
barrier	errand	preferring	terrain
carriage	horror	quarrel	terrible
carrot	irregular	quarry	tomorrow
carry	mirror	referring	worry

Exercise 8

a. **Divide the words in the word list above into syllables. What do you notice about where the syllables are divided in rr words?**

b. **Match the synonyms:**

arrest	match
carry	ashamed
conferred	mentioned
correspond	transport
errand	capture
embarrassed	discussed
preferred	enclose
referred	task
surround	submit
surrender	favoured

c. **Match the antonyms:**

narrow	reassure
irregular	glad
terrible	wide
sorry	wonderful
worry	regular

d. Write the root words of these words:

arrangement, occurrence, irregular, conferred, embarrassed, preferred

e. Find words in the word list on page 105 to match these meanings:

happening

an orange root vegetable

a container in the shape of a cylinder

water or air moving in one direction

talking bird

a stretch of land

an area where stone is mined

reflecting glass

a form of transport drawn by a horse

great fear and dislike

an angry disagreement

the next day

Double s – ss

Word list

Read and learn how to spell these words.

abcess	assume	expression	necessity
across	assure	grasshopper	permission
address	bypass	harass	possession
admission	business	impossible	possibility
assemble	discussion	massage	pressure
assign	dissolve	messenger	process
assist	encompass	missionary	unless
assorted	essay	necessary	wireless

Exercise 9

a. **Describe what these people do:**

messenger, missionary

b. **Copy the table and complete it, putting the words that follow into the first column and filling in the other columns.**

Verb	+ ed	+ ing
assemble	assembled	assembling
assign		

assign, assist, assume, assure, harass, process, massage

c. **Find words in the word list on page 106 to match each clue.**

a springing insect

check the air _____ in your tyres

you need this from your parents before you can go on an outing

you write this

these work without wires

something that is essential

hold one of these to talk about things

this is a look on your face

d. **Copy and complete these sentences with words from the word list on page 106.**

I can _____ you that it is _____ to look right and left before you walk _____ the road.

Keep your mobile phone in your _____ at all times _____ you want it to disappear.

The Olympics will _____ talented athletes from many places around the world.

_____ to the club is reserved for _____ people.

I love eating the boxes of _____ biscuits.

Double t – tt

Word list

Read and learn how to spell these words.

attach	bottle	cotton	pretty
attempt	bottom	flatten	rattle
attention	boycott	kettle	regatta
attic	butterfly	kitten	scatter
attitude	button	little	settle
attract	cattle	matter	silhouette
battle	committee	palette	spaghetti
better	cottage	pattern	written

Exercise 10

a. Add single t or double tt, or both, to these letters to make words.

aenion, commiee, wrien, aiude, cale, kien, rale, flaen, boom, bole

b. Find words in the word list above to match each of these definitions.

an insect with two pairs of wings

used to boil water

a small house

a baby's toy

a type of material

string-shaped pasta

to refuse to have anything to do with something

having an attractive face

a repetitive design

something that appears dark, but is surrounded by light

c. Use these sets of words in sentences. You can change the form of words if you need to.

For example: attempt, goal, fail – I attemp<u>ted</u> to score a goal, but fail<u>ed</u>.

1. butterfly, pretty, flutter   **3.** palette, silhouette, regatta

2. attach, kitten, little

d. Find the ten tt words hidden in this wordsearch.

B	U	T	T	O	N	Z	S	M	W
S	S	M	P	O	M	A	C	N	I
A	T	T	A	C	H	T	A	R	K
T	S	M	P	U	L	T	T	E	P
T	E	B	T	A	I	E	T	G	A
R	T	E	R	K	T	M	E	A	L
A	T	O	Z	K	T	P	R	T	E
C	L	U	Q	D	L	T	H	T	T
T	E	N	L	G	E	N	Y	A	T
D	A	T	T	I	C	G	Q	P	E

e. Choose double letters to create words that match the meaning and write the words.

a fruit: a _ _ le

use violence to harm: a _ _ ack

you wear pumps in this dance: ba _ _ et

you blow these up for parties: ba _ _ oons

something soldiers do: ba _ _ le

another word for stomach: be _ _ y

you can blow these: bu _ _ les

this could kill you: bu _ _ et

cows munch this: gra _ _

not sad: ha _ _ y

a pastime: ho _ _ y

opposite of nice: ho _ _ ible

this boils water: ke _ _ le

this involves lips: ki _ _

a baby cat: ki _ _ en

the partner of salt: pe _ _ er

a sweet dessert: pu _ _ ing

this will wet your shoes: pu _ _ le

a jigsaw: pu _ _ le

a type of puzzle: ri _ _ le

this causes sliding: sli _ _ ery

what this book is about: spe _ _ ing

a clear, hot day: su _ _ y

not the loser: wi _ _ er

Using the apostrophe correctly

Many spelling mistakes are caused by leaving out an apostrophe (') or using it incorrectly. Learn the simple rules in this chapter and avoid these mistakes.

1. Contractions

There are some words that English-speakers often join together and shorten to make a new word. For example:

I + have = I've   do + not = don't

These are called contractions and they are written with an apostrophe in place of the missing letters.

The apostrophe is written in place of the missing letters in most contractions.

When the contraction involves the word not, the apostrophe is written in place of the missing o, even if other letters are missing. For example:

can + not = can't   would + not = won't

Contractions that join a pronoun + is or a pronoun + has are both written as pronoun + 's. For example:

she + is = she's   she + has = she's

Word list			
aren't	are not	she'd	she would *or* she had
can't	cannot / can not	she'll	she will
couldn't	could not	she's	she is
didn't	did not	they'll	they will
doesn't	does not	they're	they are
don't	do not	they've	they have
hasn't	has not	wasn't	was not
haven't	have not	we'll	we will
he'd	he would *or* he had	we're	we are
he'll	he will	weren't	were not
he's	he is	we've	we have
I'd	I would *or* I had	won't	will not
I'll	I will	wouldn't	would not
I'm	I am	you'd	you would *or* you had
isn't	is not	you'll	you will
it's	it is	you're	you are
I've	I have	you've	you have

Exercise 1

a. Write each contraction out in full.

we're, wasn't, can't, don't, didn't, it's, you're, I'm, he's, we'll, they've, won't

b. Write a contraction to replace the underlined words in each sentence.

<u>It is</u> my turn.

<u>You have</u> a lovely sister.

The boy <u>does not</u> have a clue.

<u>We will</u> go to his house later.

<u>She would</u> like to go with us.

<u>They are</u> his crayons.

<u>I would</u> rather go alone.

<u>It is not</u> fair; <u>you are</u> eating much more than me.

c. Use the words in each pair in sentences to show the difference in meaning when the word is written with and without an apostrophe.

1. he'll, hell

2. she'll, shell

3. I'll, ill

4. we'll, well

5. we're, were

6. they're, there

7. she'd, shed

2. Possession

The apostrophe is also used to show that something belongs to someone or something. This is called possession. For example:

That is John's pencil.   The pencil belongs to John.

Those are the children's sweets.   The sweets belong to the children.

Those are the boys' soccer shirts.   The shirts belong to the boys.

For singular possession (when something belongs to a single person or thing) add 's. For example:

The **girl's** room.   The room belongs to the **girl**.

The **dog's** paws.   The paws belong to the **dog**.

For plural possession (when something belongs to more than one person or thing) make the noun plural first. If the plural does not end in s then add 's. For example:

The **children's** toys.   The toys belong to the **children**.

If the plural ends in s you normally just add an apostrophe, with no s. For example:

The **girls'** tennis racquets.   The tennis racquets belong to the **girls**.

When there are two or more owners only the last noun gets an apostrophe. For example:

We are going to **Jack and Jill's** house.   The house belongs to **Jack and Jill**.

Never use an apostrophe to show possession when the noun is it. (Remember: it's means it is!)

The dog wagged **its** tail.   The tree dropped **its** leaves.

Never use an apostrophe with pronouns such as his, hers, theirs, ours, yours, theirs and whose. These words already show possession so they do not need an apostrophe.

Exercise 2

a. Rewrite each phrase using an apostrophe to show the possession.

the class of the teacher

the engine of the car

the whiskers of the cat

the sister of the boy

the coat of the father

the school of my brother

the parents of my friend

the collar of the dog

the bedroom of John and Simon

➤

the house of Anne and Peter

the adventures of Tom, Dick and Harry

the games of the children

the work of the team

the houses of the men

the desks of the pupils

the titles of the books

the trunks of the elephants

the cages of the birds

the cries of the kittens

the mothers of the boys

the costumes of the actors

the ships of the navies

b. **These sentences have incorrect apostrophes. Rewrite them correctly.**

The ships' captain has his own table.

I used my mothers' phone.

John's and Cathy's garden is untidy.

Nia is waiting at the nurses' office.

The baby' shoes are under the bed.

The postmen' bags are always heavy.

The cities' air is polluted.

The ladie's committee sold tickets for the raffle.

The player's bags are in locker room.

The inspector checked all the passenger's tickets.

The girls mother's are outside.

The dog wagged it's tail.

Those shoes are her's.

➤

113

c. **Write what each phrase means.**

For example: The dog's bone   The bone belongs to the dog.

The giraffe's neck

The giraffes' feet

The cat's whiskers

The cats' paws

The boys' books

The boy's pencil

The teachers' staffroom

The principal and vice-principal's office

The birds' eggs

Extend your vocabulary

Do you remember?

◆ Vocabulary is a set of words familiar to you.

◆ Vocabulary helps you understand what you hear and read.

◆ Vocabulary helps you communicate and gain knowledge.

1. Synonyms

Synonyms are words that have the same or similar meanings.

You can use a thesaurus or a dictionary to help you find synonyms.

Finding synonyms to replace common words can make your writing more interesting.

For example: happy – cheerful.

Word list□

amazing – incredible – unbelievable – astounding – astonishing – extraordinary

big – huge – great – immense – massive – colossal

few – scarce – sparse – meagre – scant – little

many – abundance – ample – plenty – multiple – numerous

scared – terrified – petrified – frightened – afraid – alarmed

small – little – tiny – miniscule – minute – miniature

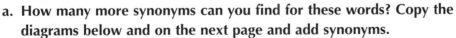

Exercise 1

a. **How many more synonyms can you find for these words? Copy the diagrams below and on the next page and add synonyms.**

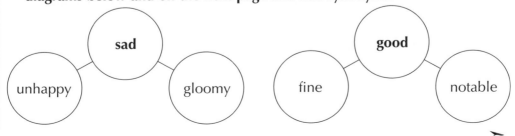

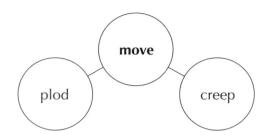

b. Rewrite these sentences, replacing the underlined words with simpler words that mean the same thing.

The unkind children <u>derided</u> the girl when she made a mistake.

I cannot concentrate as I feel <u>lethargic</u>.

I will not have more as I have had <u>an adequate sufficiency</u>.

My mother <u>compelled</u> me to attend.

The racing car travelled at great <u>velocity</u>.

c. Write shorter words that mean the same as these words.

demonstrate, emaciated, exuberant, melancholy, necessity

d. Which word is the odd one out in each group?

1. stupid   foolish   ignorant   ingenious   idiotic

2. dejected   depressed   sad   forlorn   heartened

3. start   conclude   begin   embark   commence

4. weary   exhausted   sad   fatigued   tired

5. scrawny   fat   bloated   chubby   portly

e. These words are similar, but do not mean exactly the same. Choose the most suitable word to complete each sentence.

looked, noticed, observed, gazed, watched, stared

I _____ longingly at the beautiful day and wished I wasn't stuck inside working.

We _____ television last night.

He was an eye-witness as he _____ the accident happen.

Have you _____ how much alike they are?

They _____ at the pictures for ages, but could not find one difference between them.

She _____ at the cut on her leg.

f. **Find a three-letter word that has the same or similar meaning to each of these words.**

also, attempt, conclusion, elderly, enormous, enquire, excavate, insane, lubricate, mournful, overweight, purchase, summit, weep

2. Antonyms

Antonyms are words that are opposite in meaning.

Sometimes a completely different word gives the opposite meaning.

For example: hot – cold.

Sometimes a prefix is added to the word to create the opposite.

For example: happy – unhappy.

Suffixes and prefixes may also change to create antonyms.

For example: **en**courage – **dis**courage, use**ful** – use**less.**

Word list	
add – subtract	late – early
busy – idle	like – dislike
careful – careless	narrow – wide
cheap – expensive	nearer – further
clear – murky	often – seldom
clumsy – agile	remember – forget
compliment – insult	sensible – senseless
energetic – lethargic	tight – loose
innocent – guilty	win – lose

Exercise 2

a. **Match the antonyms below and on the next page. Write sentences using each pair of words together.**

in   on

give   out

117

come	sell
up	alive
buy	death
dead	take
life	go
off	down

b. Rewrite these sentences. Replace each underlined word with an antonym.

I am going to <u>add</u> these numbers to get the answer.

The accused was found <u>guilty</u>.

We swam in very <u>cold</u> <u>clear</u> water.

I am allowed to buy <u>expensive</u> presents.

I <u>often</u> visit my grandmother in hospital.

c. Try to find an antonym for every word in this alphabetical list. Use a dictionary or thesaurus to help you.

awesome, **b**ig, **c**olourful, **d**aring, **e**xciting, **f**at, **g**lad, **h**ot, **i**nside, **j**oin, **k**ind, **l**oyal, **m**ajority, **n**eat, **o**pen, **p**lural, **q**uiet, **r**ise, **s**ame, **t**all, **u**sed, **v**ain, **w**eak, e**x**hale, **y**oung, **z**ealous

d. Add a prefix to each word to make its antonym.

clockwise, regular, proper, complete, legal

e. Change the suffix of each word to make its antonym.

hopeful, thoughtless, helpful, harmless, useful

3. Homophones

The prefix homo- means 'same'.

The suffix -phone means 'sound'.

Homophones are words that sound the same but which have different spellings and different meanings.

For example: hare and hair.

A hare is an animal that looks like a rabbit.

Hair grows on your head.

Homophones can be very confusing and can lead to spelling mistakes.

A computer spell checker will not show homophones as incorrect spellings because it does not check the meaning of the words.

Exercise 3

a. Match the words to make pairs of homophones. Check the meanings of any words you don't know in the dictionary.

ball	graphed
bald	flew
bare	meat
die	weak
draft	dye
find	stair
flu	road
flour	hear
fur	reign
graft	balled
heel	fir
here	mail
male	bear
meet	draught
piece	right
rain	threw
write	flower
rode	bawl
stare	fined
through	heal
week	peace

➤

b. **Replace the incorrect homophones in each sentence with the correct words.**

He sat buy the fire.

She preyed for piece.

Last weak I had the flew.

I road my bike to the beech.

Witch book is yours?

c. **Choose the correct words from this list to complete the following sentences.**

plain, plane, brakes, breaks, two, too, pain, pane, herd, heard, cent, scent, aloud, allowed

We are not _____ to talk in class.

In English lessons we have to read _____.

My bicycle hasn't got any _____ so I can't stop very quickly.

My sister is very clumsy, she often _____ things.

I'm tired of lending you money. I'm not giving you another _____.

Those flowers have a very strong _____.

We saw a large _____ of buffalo in the game reserve.

I _____ my favourite song on the radio.

The boy threw a stone and cracked the window _____.

He went to the doctor because he had a _____ in his chest.

We are going to the airport to catch a _____ to London.

The animals roamed across the _____.

I'm going to school. Are you coming _____?

We will be home at _____ o'clock.

d. **Write sentences using the words in each pair to show the difference in their meaning.**

1. weather, whether   4. board, bored

2. principal, principle   5. coarse, course

3. past, passed   6. fair, fare

e. **Find the words that have been used incorrectly in each sentence. Write the correct words.**

The medals were made of 9 carrot gold.

The fishermen picked muscles from the rocks.

When you collect data you have to find a suitable sauce.

After the bride walked down the isle, the bridle party went to the park to have photos taken.

My sister and I like to wonder around the mall.

Put your bags down over their.

4. Homonyms

Homonyms are words that have the same spelling and the same pronunciation but which can have different meanings depending on how they are used. For example:

My dog has a very loud **bark**.

The **bark** of the tree was covered in moss.

Exercise 4

One meaning of each word has been given. Use your dictionary and your general knowledge to find one more meaning for each word. Copy and complete the table.

Homonym	Meaning 1	Meaning 2
ball	formal dance	
bat	flying rodent	
cricket	insect	
cold	illness	
date	fruit from a palm tree	
fair	just, treating everyone the same	
glasses	drinking containers	
jam	fruit spread for bread	
record	write down	
second	unit of time	
spring	coiled metal object	
tip	money given to a waiter	
trip	fall over something	

5. Homographs

Homographs are words that have the same spelling but which have a different pronunciation and meaning. For example:

Every night I **wind** up my alarm clock. (wind rhymes with kind)

There is a very strong **wind** blowing. (wind rhymes with pinned)

The fishing weights were made of **lead**. (lead rhymes with bed)

I will **lead** the way. (lead rhymes with bead)

The way you pronounce the word depends on its meaning and how it is used.

Word list			
bass	invalid	present	subject
bow	lead	project	tear
close	live	record	use
conduct	minute	read	wind
content	object	row	wound
desert	perfect	second	
does	polish	sow	

Exercise 5

a. **Read the words in the word list above aloud. Try to find at least two ways of pronouncing each word.**

b. **Find all the correct meanings of each homograph.**

bass	type of fish	musical instrument	a deep sound
bow	lean down	weapon used with an arrow	ribbon
close	nearby	shut	almost
conduct	behaviour	lead an orchestra	type of pipe
content	try very hard	satisfied	information inside a book
desert	leave behind	dry, sandy region	pudding
does	female deer	present tense of do	amount of medicine
invalid	not true	not valuable	a sick person

c. **One pronunciation of each word is given. Write a sentence to show what the word means when it is pronounced in that way.**

lead – rhymes with bed

live – rhymes with give

minute – pronounced my-newt

object – emphasis on ob–, **ob**-ject

perfect – emphasis on fect – per-**fect**

Polish – emphasis on Po, **Po**-lish (and spelt with a capital p)

present – emphasis on pres, **pres**-ent

read – rhymes with red

d. **Two definitions of each word are given. Find the word in the word list on page 122 that matches both.**

straight line or argument

plant seeds or female pig

position in a race or part of a minute

beating a time in a race or writing something down

task or predict for the future

e. **Choose which of these homographs matches each meaning that follows.**

subject, tear, use, wind, wound

rip

moving air

wrapped around something

purpose for something

under the rule of another

6. Gender words

Gender tells you whether someone or something is male or female.

Sometimes different words are used for male and female.

> For example: man – woman.

Sometimes the same word is used for both male and female. This is known as common gender.

> For example: baby, friend, chef.

Neuter gender refers to things that are neither male nor female.

> For example: desk, book.

Word list

Masculine	Feminine	Common	Neuter
bachelor	spinster	cousin	book
boy	girl	dentist	car
brother	sister	doctor	computer
brother-in-law	sister-in-law	teenager	egg
father	mother		
gentleman	lady		
grandfather	grandmother		
grandson	granddaughter		
headmaster	headmistress		
king	queen		
man	woman		
nephew	niece		
sir	madam		
son	daughter		
uncle	aunt		

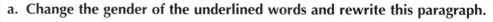

Exercise 6

a. Change the gender of the underlined words and rewrite this paragraph.

My <u>father</u> and <u>uncle</u> met me at the airport. My <u>brother</u> wasn't with them because <u>he</u> was at school. My <u>mother</u> was visiting my <u>grandmother</u> in hospital. I feel sorry for <u>her</u>. <u>She</u> is very sick.

b. Make two columns headed Masculine and Feminine. Find the matching gender words and write them in the correct column.

daughter, prince, waiter, bridegroom, duchess, actress, mayoress, host, widower, congresswoman, congressman, princess, bride, actor, widow, son, hostess, mayor, duke, waitress

c. Many professions have different words for male and female. Write down as many as you can think of.

For example: actor – actress.

d. Many professions have adopted one common gender to refer to males and females. Write down as many as you can think of.

For example: accountant.

e. Find words in the word list on page 124 that match these definitions.

my sister's husband

an unmarried man

a female ruler

my father's brother's daughter

I call my mother's sister this

Animals also have different genders.

Word list			
Male		**Female**	
billy-goat	fox	nanny-goat	vixen
boar (pig)	gander	sow	goose
buck	lion	doe	lioness
bull	peacock	cow	peahen
bull-elephant	ram	cow-elephant	ewe
cock	stallion (adult horse)	hen	mare
colt (young horse)	tom-cat	filly	tabby-cat
drake		duck	

Exercise 7

Find the matching pairs.

stallion	sow
ram	filly
gander	doe
bull	ewe
boar	goose
colt	cow
fox	duck
drake	mare
buck	vixen

7. Diminutives

Young animals have different names from adult animals. We sometimes call these young animals diminutives. Diminutive refers to something small or young.

Word list

Adult	Young	Adult	Young
bear	cub	bird	nestling, fledg(e)ling
buck, deer	fawn	bull, cow	calf
butterfly	caterpillar	cat	kitten
cock, hen	chicken	dog	puppy
duck	duckling	eagle	eaglet
eel	elver	elephant	calf
fish	fry	fox	cub
frog	tadpole	goat	kid
goose	gosling	horse	foal
kangaroo	joey	lion	cub
owl	owlet	pig	piglet
salmon	parr	sheep	lamb
swan	cygnet	whale	calf

Exercise 8

a. Copy and complete these sentences.

A young fox is a _____.

A young fish is a _____.

An adult calf is a _____, _____, _____ or a _____.

A young eel is an _____.

A young owl is an _____.

A young frog is a _____.

An adult parr is a _____.

An adult joey is a _____.

A young goat is a _____.

A young butterfly or moth is a _____.

b. Match the adults and their young.

bear	gosling
deer	eaglet
bird	piglet
eagle	foal
lion	fawn
sheep	cub
swan	duckling
goose	chicken
horse	lamb
hen	cub
pig	kitten
duck	nestling
cat	puppy
dog	cygnet

8. Animal sounds

We use specific words to name the sounds that different animals make.

Many of these words sound like the noise the animal makes.

Read and learn how to spell these words.

Word list			
Animal	**Sound**	**Animal**	**Sound**
apes	gibber	bears	growl
bees	buzz, hum	beetles	drone
bulls	bellow	cats	meow, purr
chickens	peep	cows	low, moo
crickets	chirp	crows	caw
dogs	bark, growl	donkeys	bray
doves	coo	ducks	quack
eagles	scream	elephants	trumpet
frogs	croak	geese	cackle, hiss
goats, sheep	bleat	hens	cackle, cluck
hyenas	laugh, scream	lions	roar
monkeys	chatter	owls	hoot
pigs	grunt	snakes	hiss
turkeys	gobble	wolves	howl

Exercise 9

a. Copy and complete these sentences about the sounds animals make.

An elephant _____.

A donkey _____.

A _____ cackles and hisses.

A monkey _____.

An _____ screams.

A pig _____.

An _____ gibbers.

A snake _____.

A _____ howls.

A frog _____.

b. Alliteration is the repetition of the beginning sounds of words.

For example: **ch**eeky **ch**ickens **ch**eeping and **ch**irping.

Write examples of alliteration using the following animals and sounds.

For example: seagulls – scream: **s**eagulls **s**cream **s**ensationally.

bees – buzz

bulls – bellow

crows – caw

crickets – chirp

c. Identify the words related to each animal family and write them in a table like the one below.

boar, mare, cub, bleat, trumpet, kid, lioness, stallion, grunt, foal, lion, billy-goat, bull-elephant, roar, calf, sow, nanny-goat, cow-elephant, neigh, piglet

Masculine	Feminine	Diminutive	Sound
bull	cow	calf	low

d. Match each animal to the sound it makes.

chickens	howl
doves	growl
hyenas	low
turkeys	drone
bears	quack
beetles	hiss
ducks	coo
cows	hoot
hens	gobble
owls	laugh
snakes	peep
wolves	cackle

First aid for common spelling problems

1. Commonly confused words

Spelling problems can result if you confuse two words that sound similar or the same but which have different spellings and meanings, for example: desert and dessert or pair and pear. Learning some words that are commonly confused in English and knowing their meanings can help you to spell and use them correctly.

Word list

Commonly confused words	Meanings
accept	allow, receive
except	leave out
advice	an opinion that you give or receive
advise	to give someone advice
affect	to influence
effect	the result of something else
a lot	many
alot	this word does not exist!
all ready	everyone or everything is ready
already	by this time
altar	a place of worship
alter	to change
altogether	entirely
all together	as a group
brake	stop
break	separate into parts, destroy
choose	make a choice (present tense)
chose	to have made a choice (past tense)
cite	to refer to, quote
sight	vision, your sense of seeing
site	place where something happens
desert	dry sandy place; to leave behind
dessert	pudding
formally	officially
formerly	before
its	belonging to it (possessive)
it's	it is (contraction)
know	to understand, be familiar with
no	negative, opposite of yes ➤

Commonly confused words	Meanings
lead	heavy metal; to direct or show the way
led	showed the way (past tense of to lead)
lie	to lie down; to tell an untruth; an untruth
lay	to put something down
lose	to misplace; opposite of to win
loose	not tight
pair	two
pear	a fruit
pare	to peel something
passed	past tense of to pass
past	a previous time; a position that is further away
peace	tranquillity, opposite of war
piece	part of, slice
plain	ordinary
plane	flat surface; aeroplane
principal	person in charge of a school
principle	a general rule; behaviour
quiet	soft, not noisy
quite	very, rather
right	correct; direction opposite to left
write	to make notes by hand
rite	ceremony
stationary	standing still
stationery	paper, pens and other writing tools
steel	a metal
steal	to take something that is not yours
than	used to compare
then	at that time; next
their	belonging to them
there	a location or place
they're	they are (contraction)
threw	tossed (past tense of to throw)
through	from one end of something to the other
to	toward
too	also; excessively
two	2 ➤

Commonly confused words	Meanings
who	pronoun, refers to a person
which	pronoun used to talk about things, never used with people
that	refers to a group of things, or a group of people
who's	who is (contraction)
whose	used to add information about a person or ask who owns something
your	belonging to you (possessive)
you're	you are (contraction)

Exercise 1

a. Find the word that matches the meaning.

past tense of to throw	threw	through	
writing materials	stationery	stationary	
correct	right	rite	write
a fruit	pair	pear	pare
hard silver metal	steel	steal	
moved around something	past	passed	
place where a battle took place	sight	site	

b. Rewrite each sentence choosing the correct word from the brackets.

He walked (past / passed) the window.

The traffic was (stationary / stationery) because of an accident.

(They're / Their) waiting for a bus.

Only (too / two) students were late for class.

Please (accept / except) my apologies for being late.

The teacher sent the late-comers to the (principal / principle).

I hate it when I (lose / loose) my pencil.

She has (alot / a lot) of shoes.

➤

c. **Look up the meanings of these words in your dictionary. Write sentences to show their meanings.**

1. rein	rain		**6.** aloud	allowed	
2. sale	sail		**7.** larva	lava	
3. ore	oar		**8.** board	bored	
4. might	mite		**9.** waste	waist	
5. isle	aisle				

d. **Correct these sentences.**

She cut her foot on a peace of glass.

I read the hole book last week.

An eagle is a bird of pray.

She felt sick, so she went to lay down.

My eyes are as heavy as led.

It's all ready four o'clock.

We are going to have ice cream for desert.

Be careful or you will brake something.

2. Words that are often spelt incorrectly

Word list

academic	calendar	forehead	paraffin	separate
access	century	frequently	parallel	sincerely
accommodation	changeable	guarantee	parliament	successful
across	committed	government	particularly	technique
aerial	continuous	guard	possess	tomorrow
annual	definitely	height	preferred	tongue
anxious	desperate	immediately	proceed	thorough
arctic	disappeared	knowledge	queue	vaccinate
assassin	discussion	laboratory	receive	vacuum
beginning	embarrass	length	recognise	veterinary
behaviour	emphasis	literature	recommend	Wednesday
bicycle	exaggerate	necessary	rhyme	yacht
business	fascination	occasion	rhythm	zoology

133

Exercise 2

a. Read the words in the word list on page 133. Underline any that you have difficulty with. Add these to your personal dictionary and learn to spell them using whichever method you find easiest.

b. Which word is spelt correctly in each group?

1.	acomodation	accommodation	accomodation
2.	bycycle	bicicle	bicycle
3.	continnous	continuous	continueous
4.	definitly	definetley	definitely
5.	desparate	desperete	desperate
6.	embarass	embarrass	embarras
7.	forhead	fourhead	forehead
8.	lenthg	length	lenght
9.	ocassion	occasion	occassion
10.	parallell	parrallel	parallel
11.	seperete	separate	separete
12.	tomorow	tommorow	tomorrow
13.	yahct	yacht	yaught

c. Choose a word from the word list on page 133 to complete each sentence.

We took our sick dog to the _____ clinic.

We received a two year _____ when we bought a new television.

The technician came and put up a special _____ on the roof so we could get good television reception.

That store gives good service. I would highly _____ them.

I'll have to check the _____ to see what day of the week that is.

It was not so big! Don't _____.

We had to stand in a _____ for a very long time before we were served.

I _____ hope that he gets better soon.

➤

d. Make your own wordsearch using ten words from the word list on page 133.

Write the words horizontally, vertically or diagonally in a grid like the one below.

Fill the empty blocks with other letters.

Give your wordsearch to a friend and try to find each other's words.

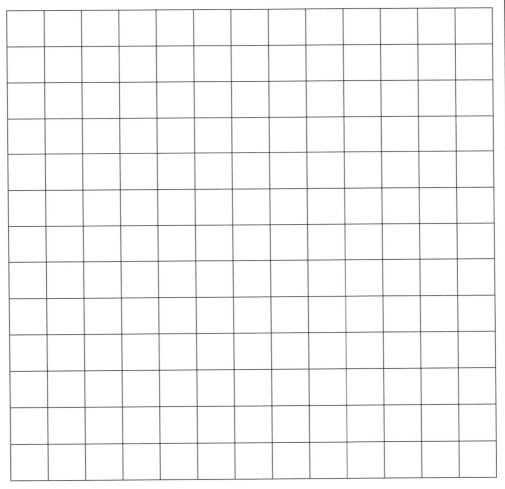

e. Give each other a spelling test to check that you can both spell the words in your wordsearches.

Useful words to know

You will use a lot of the words in these lists in everyday life. Make sure you know how to spell them correctly.

1. Time

Word list

Read and learn how to spell these words.

Days of the week	Months of the year	Describing time
Sunday	January	AD – Anno Domini (Latin for 'in the year of the Lord')
Monday	February	BC – Before Christ
Tuesday	March	a.m. – ante meridiem (Latin for 'before noon')
Wednesday	April	p.m. – post meridiem (Latin for 'after noon')
Thursday	May	
Friday	June	
Saturday	July	yesterday, today, tomorrow
	August	day, night
	September	sunrise, dawn, sunset, dusk, twilight
	October	morning, midday, afternoon, evening, midnight
	November	second, minute, hour
	December	year, leap year, decade, century, millennium

Adverbs of time

annually

eventually

immediately

instantly

lately

previously

punctually

recently

Exercise 1

a. Match each time word to its definition.

minute	just before the sky becomes dark at night
dawn	first light of the day as the sun rises
day	sixty seconds
dusk	366 days
decade	sixty minutes
hour	twenty-four hours
millennium	a hundred years
p.m.	after noon
a.m.	365 days
century	ten years
year	a thousand years
leap year	before noon

b. Copy and complete the rhyme.

Thirty days hath _____,

April, June, and _____;

All the rest have _____,

Save _____, with twenty-eight days clear,

And twenty-nine each _____ year.

c. Write an activity you do on these days of the week.

Sunday:

Monday:

Friday:

Saturday:

d. Rewrite the paragraph using the correct word in the brackets.

(Yesterday / Tomorrow) I spent all (day / night) learning for a vocabulary test. In 2030 (BC / AD) I do not plan to work from (Saturday / Monday) to (Sunday / Friday). I want to be able to fish from (dawn / dusk) to (dawn / dusk). I will wake at 5(a.m. / p.m.) to watch the (sunset / sunrise) and make every (minute / second) of every (minute / second) count.

137

2. Measurement

Word list

Read and learn how to spell these words.

Metric measurements						Imperial measurements	
millimetre	mm	milligram	mg	millilitre	ml	dozen	doz
centimetre	cm	centigram	cg	centilitre	cl	inch	in
decimetre	dm	decigram	dg	decilitre	dl	foot	ft
metre	m	gram	g	litre	l	yard	yd
hectometre	hm	hectogram	hg	hectolitre	hl	ounce	oz
kilometre	km	kilogram	kg	kilolitre	kl	pound	lb
						pint	pt
						quart	qt
						gallon	gal

Exercise 2

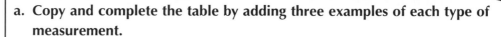

a. Copy and complete the table by adding three examples of each type of measurement.

Measurement of length	Measurement of weight	Measurement of volume

b. Copy and complete the sentences.

A _____ is a group of twelve.

A _____ is equal to 30.48 cm or 12 in.

A _____ is equal to 16 oz and 0.45 kg.

A _____ is equal to 10 mm.

A _____ is equal to 1000 g.

A _____ is equal to 100 cm.

A _____ is equal to 1/10 of a metre.

A _____ is equal to 100 grams.

c. **Cover the word list on page 138 and write the correct spelling for each pair of words.**

millimeter	millimetre	milillitre	millilitre
centemetre	centimetre	kilometre	kilomitre
decigram	desigram	hectametre	hectometre
hektogram	hectogram	miligram	milligram
killolitre	kilolitre	liter	litre

3. Onomatopoeic words

Onomatopoeic words sound like what they are describing. Using onomatopoeic words in your writing will help to make it more descriptive.

Word list

buzz	gurgle	sizzle	thump
chirp	howl	slither	tinkle
clatter	murmur	slurp	whip
crash	quack	splatter	whisper
creak	roar	squash	whistle
flutter	rustle	thud	zoom

Exercise 3

a. **Write a description using as many of the onomatopoeic words in the word list above as possible. You will need to add the suffixes -ed and -ing to some of the words. Describe one of the following:**

an accident   a class party   a messy eater

b. **Copy and complete the sentences below by adding these onomatopoeic words to them.**

creaked, fluttering, splattered, rustle, clatter, whistled, crash, roaring, howled, thud, slither, sizzled

The _____ wind _____ through the trees making the leaves _____.

With a loud _____ and a _____, the dishes landed on the floor.

The oil _____ all over the stove as the bacon _____ away.

The boy _____ as he saw a snake _____ between the _____ washing.

There was a _____ on the stairs and then the door _____ open.

c. **Write your own words to describe the sound of:**

waves in the sea   a storm

4. Words that describe speech

These words describe how you say something. Use them instead of said to make your writing more expressive.

Word list

chuckled	screamed	announced	declared
exclaimed	shrieked	advised	denied
laughed	snarled	agreed	insisted
moaned	sniggered	admitted	objected
mumbled	sobbed	confessed	protested

Exercise 4

a. **Try to say the sentence 'I am going too.' out loud in all of the different ways described by the words in the word list above.**

b. **Replace the word said with one of these words in each of the sentences below.**

shrieked, agreed, sniggered, insisted, moaned, laughed, confessed, denied, announced, snarled

'I did steal the money,' <u>said</u> the criminal.

'That is the funniest story I have ever heard,' <u>said</u> Dad.

'And you expect me to believe that tall tale,' <u>said</u> Mum.

'I'm in agony,' <u>said</u> my sister.

'It's alive!' <u>said</u> my cousin as she sprang on the table.

'I did not do it,' <u>said</u> my brother.

'You had better be careful or I'll show you who's boss later,' <u>said</u> the bully.

'You will write a science test on Wednesday,' <u>said</u> my teacher. ➤

'You have to take this one,' <u>said</u> my friend.

'I think you are right,' <u>said</u> my grandmother.

c. Write words to match these clues.

to speak quietly without opening your mouth much

to shout out loudly and suddenly

to complain or object strongly against something

to say something with a quiet laugh

to speak while crying

d. Use these words to complete the sentences below.

declared, admitted, protested, advised

'If you want to be prepared for the test, you need to learn how to spell the words,' _____ my mother.

'I do not want to go,' _____ my nephew.

'That is how it is going to be from now on,' _____ my grandfather.

'I suppose I should start studying,' _____ my niece.

5. Words that describe movement

These words describe ways of moving. Use them to make your writing more descriptive.

Word list			
amble	frolic	plunge	squirm
bob	glide	pounce	stagger
bounce	hobble	prance	trot
bustle	jostle	skip	trudge
crawl	leap	skulk	waddle
creep	loiter	slide	wallow
dawdle	lope	slither	weave
drift	lurch	slouch	whirl
droop	plod	soar	wriggle

Exercise 5

a. Match these movements and descriptions.

amble	to jump up and down
bob	to move very quietly
bounce	to move slowly and reluctantly
bustle	to hurry around getting things organised
crawl	to walk in a slow relaxed way
creep	to move in a lively and carefree way
dawdle	to move on your hands and knees
drift	to bounce up and down frequently especially in water
droop	move aimlessly in an unforced, unhurried way
frolic	to move in a dejected way with your head and body sagging limply

b. Match these synonyms.

limp	glide
slump	hobble
fly	jostle
jump	stagger
float	pounce
shove	slouch
spin	soar
squirm	whirl
stumble	wriggle

c. Act out these movements.

trot, trudge, waddle, wallow, pounce, prance, skip, skulk, slide, slither, stagger, squirm

d. Use a dictionary to help you describe these movements.

loiter, lope, lurch, plod, plunge

6. Colours

You may know that the primary colours are red, blue and yellow.

You may also know the colours of the rainbow are red, orange, yellow, green, blue, indigo and violet.

You can remember the colours of the rainbow and their order using the mnemonic ROYGeeBIV or VIBGYOR.

There are many other colours too. How many of the ones in the list do you know?

Word list			
auburn	crimson	lemon	pink
azure	ebony	lilac	purple
beige	emerald	lime	red
black	fuchsia	magenta	rose
bronze	gold	mahogany	sapphire
brown	green	maroon	scarlet
carmine	grey	mauve	silver
cobalt	indigo	mint	turquoise
copper	ivory	mustard	violet
coral	khaki	navy	white
cream	lavender	orange	yellow

Exercise 6

a. Write a list of the shades of blue.

b. Write a list of the shades of red.

c. Use coloured pencils to show the shades of ten colours in the list above. Write the names next to the colours.

d. Copy and complete this table by listing five examples of colours that match each heading.

Brilliant (bright, vivid) colours	Drab (dull, dowdy) colours	Gaudy (flashy, showy) colours

e. Write headings for these lists of colours. Start with the words 'Shades of …'.

1. cream, ivory, white

2. emerald, lime, mint

3. violet, mauve, lavender

4. silver, gold, bronze

5. khaki, mustard, beige

f. With what do you associate these colours?

For example: red – blood, anger, danger.

white, black, grey, blue, green, yellow, purple, orange

g. Copy and complete these sentences with interesting comparisons of your own.

For example: As red as blood droplets on snow.

As white as _____.

As black as _____.

As pink as _____.

As purple as _____.

As yellow as _____.

As gold as _____.

As silver as _____.

As turquoise as _____.

7. Words used in lessons

School subjects often use special vocabulary. It is important to know what these key terms mean and to be able to spell them correctly in tests and examinations.

Word list

Mathematics	General science	Biology
million	acid	animals
billion	alkali	bacteria
	apparatus	biodegradable
addition	atom	biology
subtraction	atmosphere	carnivore
multiplication	boiling	cell
division	carbohydrate	chlorophyll
factor	carbon dioxide	classification
multiple	catalyst	conservation
	chemical	decompose
decimal	chemistry	deforestation
denominator	colour	digestion
factor	compound	disease
fraction	convection	drought
multiple	crystal	ecology
numerator	current	environment
percentage	dissolve	excretion
ratio	electricity	extinct
	element	food chain
average	energy	fossil
axis (axes)	expansion	habitat
data	experiment	herbivore
interval	filter	invertebrate
mean	float	laboratory
median	force	life cycle
mode	formula	locomotion
range	friction	mammal
scale	gravity	metamorphosis
	hydrogen	microscope
acute	laboratory	nutrition
adjacent	material	omnivore
angle	measurement	organ
area	mineral	organism
capacity	molecule	photosynthesis
circle	motion	pollution

Mathematics

circumference
cone
congruent
cube
cylinder
diagonal
diameter
edge
heptagon
hexagon
horizontal
hypotenuse
kite
line
net
obtuse
oval
parallel
parallelogram
pentagon
perimeter
perpendicular
prism
pyramid
radius
rectangle
reflex
rhombus
right angle
scalene
semicircle
sphere
square
symmetrical
trapezium
triangle
vertical

General science

nitrogen
oxygen
ozone
particle
physics
pressure
reaction
reflect
resistance
speed
substance
synthetic
temperature
thermometer
translucent
transparent
vacuum
vapour
volume

Biology

protein
recycle
reproduce
respiration
species
skeleton
vertebrate
virus
vitamin
warm-blooded
water
zoology

Word list

History

ally
ancient
artifact / artefact
border
chronology
civilisation
conflict
culture
discovery
emancipation
empire
event
evidence
govern
government
historian
independence
international
invention
military
opinion
political
religion
revolution
slavery
society
source
timeline
trade
voyages
war

Geography

Africa
agriculture
altitude
America
Antarctic
Arctic
Asia
atlas
Australia
capital
cartographer
climate
communications
compass
continent
cyclone
desert
directions
drought
earthquake
Equator
Europe
export
forestry
hemisphere
horizon
hurricane
island
landform
latitude
longitude

meridian
mountain
north
ocean
planet
population
precipitation
region
relief
resources
rural
season
south
temperate
tornado
tropics
tundra
urban
water cycle
weather

Spelling list

a lot
abacus
about
abscess
abstain
abstract
abundance
academic
academically
accede
accelerate
accent
accept
acceptance
access
accessorise
accident
accidentally
acclaim
accommodate
accommodation
accomplish
accordion
account
accountant
accumulate
accurate
accuse
accustomed
ace
ache
achieve
acid
acorn
across
act
active
actor
actual

acute
add
addict
addition
address
adhere
adjacent
adjective
admission
admitted
advance
advantageous
adverb
advertise
advice
advise
advised
aerial
aerobics
aeroplane
aerosol
affable
affair
affect
affectionate
affix
afford
afraid
Africa
after
afternoon
age
agent
agile
agonise
agreed
agriculture
aircraft
alarmed

alive
alkali
all ready
all together
allergic
alley
allow
ally
alphabet
already
altar
alter
alteration
although
altitude
altogether
amazing
ambition
ambitious
amble
America
amount
ample
amplifier
analyse
anchor
ancient
angle
angrier
animal, animals
Anno Domini / AD
announce
announced
annoying
annual
annually
another
Antarctic
ante meridiem / a.m.

antenatal

antenna, antennae

anticlimax

anticlockwise

antiseptic

anxious

apart

apes

aphid

apologise

apparatus

appear

appearance

apple

April

architect

arctic / Arctic

area

aren't / are not

argue

argument

arm

army

arrangement

array

arrest

arrive

art

article

artifact / artefact

Asia

asparagus

ass

assassin

assemble

assembly

assign

assist

assistance

assorted

assume

assure

astonishing

astounding

atlas

atmosphere

atom

attach

attachment

attempt

attention

attentive

attic

attitude

attract

attractive

auburn

August

aunt

Australia

author

autumn

avenue

average

avoid

award

awful

axis, axes

azure

baby

bachelor

back

backpack

bacteria

baffle

bagful

baggage

baker

banjos

banner

baptise

bar

bargain

bark

barracks

barrel

barrier

bass

bat

battle

beach

beaker

bear, bears

beautiful

beautifully

because

bedroom

bees

beetles

Before Christ / BC

began

beggar

begged

beginning

behaviour

beige

belief, beliefs

believe

bell

bellow

benefited

better

biathlon

bicycle

big

billion

billy-goat

binocular

biodegradable

biology

bird

birth

black

bleat

bless

blizzard

blossom

blue

bluff

boar
bob
boil
boiling
book
border
borrow
boss
bottle
bottom
bought
bounce
bound
boundary
bow
box
boxer
boy
boycott
boyfriend
brace
brake
branch
bravely
bravery
bray
bread
break
breeze
bribery
bridge
brief
brilliance
brilliant
broccoli
bronze
broom
brother
brother-in-law
brought
brown
browse
bruise

buck
budget
buffalo, buffaloes
bug
bull, bulls
bull-elephant
bullet
bun
bunny
bureau, bureaux / bureaus
bus
bush
business
bustle
busy
butterfly
button
buzz
bypass
cab
cabbage
cackle
cactus, cactuses / cacti
calendar
calf, calves
call
called
camel
camper
campfire
campus
can
can't / cannot / can not
cancel
cannibal
capacity
capital
cappuccinos
captive
car
carbohydrate
carbon
carbon dioxide

career
careful
careless
cargoes
carmine
carnivore
carpet
carpeting
carriage
carrier
carrot
carry
cart
cartographer
cashier
casual
cat, cats
catalyst
catch
caterpillar
cattle
caught
cause
cautious
caw
cede
ceiling
celery
cell
cellos
cement
cemetery
census
centennial
centigram
centilitre
centimetre
centre
century
certain
chain
chair
chalk

challenge

chameleon

champion

change

changeable

channel

chapter

chase

chatter

cheap

cheat

check

cheer

cheese

cheetah

chemical

chemist

chemistry

chess

chew

chicken, chickens

chief, chiefs

child, children

chilly

chimpanzee

chin

chip

chirp

chlorophyll

choose

chorus

chose

Christian

Christmas

chrome

chronic

chronology

chrysanthemum

chuckle

chuckled

church

churchyard

cider

cinema

cinnamon

circle

circumference

circus

cite

civilisation

civilise

class

classification

clatter

clear

click

cliff, cliffs

climate

climb

climber

clock

close

clothes

cloud

clown

cluck

clue

clumsy

clutter

coat

cobalt

cock

code

coffee

collect

college

collide

collision

colonise

colossal

colour

colt

comfortable

comic

command

commence

comment

commit

commitment

committed

committee

common

communications

compass

competence

competent

competitive

compile

complain

complete

compliment

compound

computer

concede

conclude

conclusion

conduct

cone

conference

conferring

confessed

confidence

conflict

confuse

confusion

congruent

connect

connive

conscience

consensus

conservation

construct

constructive

construe

content

contextual

continent

continue

continuous

contract	criticise	decimal
contrive	croak	decimetre
control	crocodile	decision
convection	cross	deck
convenient	crowd	declared
conveyed	crown	decompose
conveying	crows	decorate
coo	crust	decoration
cope	cry	deduct
copper	crystal	deer
coral	cub	defect
corn	cube	definitely
corner	cucumber	deforestation
correct	cue	defrost
correction	culture	delayed
correspond	cunning	delicious
corrupt	curios	delivery
cottage	current	denied
cotton	cut	denominator
cough	cute	dentist
couldn't / could not	cyclone	descend
council	cygnet	desert
councillor	cylinder	desiccated
count	dance	despair
country	danger	desperate
courage	dangerous	dessert
courageous	dark	destroyed
cousin	data	destructive
cow, cows	daughter	detain
cow-elephant	daughter-in-law	devise
coward	dawdle	diagonal
crash	dawn	diameter
crawl	day	dictionary
crayon	dazzle	didn't / did not
creak	de-stress	die, dice
cream	decade	differ
creative	deceive	difference
creep	decelerate	different
cricket	December	difficult
crickets	decent	digestion
crime	decide	digestive
crimson	decigram	dinner
crisis, crises	decilitre	dinosaur

direct
directions
dirty
disappearance
disappeared
disappointment
disarm
disbelief
discovery
discus
discussion
disease
dish
dishonest
dislike
dissolve
distraught
division
dizzy
dock
doctor
document
dodge
doe
does
doesn't / does not
dog, dogs
dolphin
dominoes
don't / do not
donkey, donkeys
door
doubt
dough
doves
dozen
dragon
drake
dramatise
draw
drawing
dress
drift

drone
droop
drought
dual
duck, ducks
duckling
due
dull
dusk
dwarf, dwarfs
dyeing
dying
eagle, eagles
eaglet
early
earth
earthquake
ease
ebony
eccentric
echo, echoes
ecology
edge
edible
editor-in-chief
eel
effect
efficient
effort
egg
eight
either
electricity
elegance
elegant
element
elementary
elephant, elephants
elver
emancipation
embarrass
embarrassed
emerald

emphasis
emphasise
empire
employment
emptiness
empty
emptying
encompass
energetic
energetically
energise
energy
engagement
engaging
engineer
enjoyment
enormous
enough
entertain
environment
equal
Equator
errand
essay
ethnic
eucalyptus
Europe
evening
event
eventually
evidence
ewe
exaggerate
example
exceed
except
excitement
exciting
exclaimed
excretion
exercise
exhaust
expansion

expensive	flexible	frequent
experiment	flick	frequently
explain	float	friction
explanation	flock	Friday
export	flower	friend
expression	flue	frightened
extinct	fluffy	frog
extract	flutter	frolic
extraordinary	fly	frolicking
eye	foal	frontier
face	focal	fry
factor	focus	fuchsia
factual	food chain	fulfil
fail	foot, feet	fulfilled
fair	forbid	fungus
familiarise	forbidden	funnel
famous	force	further
fantastic	forehead	fuss
fascinate	forestry	futile
fascination	forget	fuzzy
fashionable	forgetting	gadget
father	forgive	gallery
father-in-law	forgotten	gallon
fault	form	gallop
fawn	formally	galloping
February	former	gander
feint	formerly	garden
fertile	formula, formulae	gardener
fever	fortunate	gas
few	fortunately	gauge
field	fortune	gauze
fierce	forward	geese
fighter	fossil	gem
fighting	fought	generous
file	foul	generously
filly	found	gentle
filter	fox	gentleman
finite	fraction	geography
fish	fragile	germ
fitting	fragment	giant
fizz	fraught	gibber
flatten	freeze	gimmick
fledgling / fledgeling	freight	ginger

giraffe	grunt	heptagon
girl	guarantee	her
gladly	guard	herbivore
gladness	guess	herd
glass	guilty	here
glasses	gull	heroes
glide	gum	heroic
glory	gunned	hexagon
glue	gurgle	hiccup
goat, goats	gutter	hippopotamus,
gobble	habitat	hippopotamuses /
going	half, halves	hippopotami
gold	halos / haloes	hiss
good	hammer	historian
goods	hammock	hobble
goose, geese	happily	holiday
gorgeous	harass	homeless
gorilla	harbour	honour
gosling	hard	honourable
govern	harmless	hoof, hoofs / hooves
government	hasn't / has not	hoot
gracious	hat	hopeful
gradual	hatch	hoping
graffiti	haunt	hopped
gram	haven't / have not	horizon
grammar	he'd / he would / he had	horizontal
granddad	he'll / he will	horrible
granddaughter	he's / he is	horror
grandfather	head	horse
grandmother	headmaster	hostage
grandson	headmistress	hostel
graph	headquarters	hour
grass	hear	house
grasshopper	heavily	how
grateful	heavy	however
gravity	hectogram	howl
great	hectolitre	huff
green	hectometre	huge
grey	height	hugged
grief	heir	hum
grim	helpful	humorous
grin	hemisphere	hurricane
growl	hen, hens	hutch

hydrogen	inner	jog
hyenas	innocent	joker
hygiene	insincere	jostle
hyphen	insisted	journey
hypotenuse	instantly	joyful
I'd / I would / I had	instead	judge
I'll / I will	instinct	judgement
I'm / I am	instruct	jug
I've / I have	instrument	July
icicle	insult	jump
identical	intellectual	jumped
idle	intelligent	June
idolise	intercede	junk
igloos	interesting	just
illegal	interfere	kangaroo
illiterate	international	keen
imaginary	interpret	keep
immature	interval	kennel
immediate	invalid	kerb
immediately	invention	kettle
immense	invertebrate	key
immobile	irrational	keyboard
immune	irregular	khaki
impact	irritable	kick
imperfect	island	kid
impolite	isn't / is not	kilogram
importance	issue	kilolitre
important	it's / it is	kilometre
impossible	its	kilos
improvement	ivory	kind
inattentive	jack	king
inch	jacket	kiss
incomplete	jam	kitchen
inconvenient	January	kite
incorrect	jar	kitten
incredible	jazz	knife, knives
independence	jealous	know
indigo	jeer	knowledge
indirect	jewel	label
industry	jewellery	laboratory
inexpensive	jive	ladder
infinite	job	lady
ink	joey	lady-in-waiting

lamb	literary	manhood
landform	literate	mannequin
language	literature	manual
lap	litre	manufacture
lard	little	many
large	live	march
larva, larvae	liver	March
lass	loaf, loaves	mare
late	local	mark
lately	locate	market
latitude	location	maroon
laugh	locomotion	marvellous
laughed	log	mass
laundry	logic	massage
lavender	logically	massive
law	loiter	mat
lawyer	longitude	match
lay	looker-on	material
lead	looking	mathematics
leaf, leaves	loose	matter
leap	lope	mauve
leap year	lord	May
led	lose	meagre
legend	loss	mean
lemon	louse	meanness
length	low	meanwhile
less	luck	measurement
lethargic	lurch	mechanic
library	luxurious	median
lice	luxury	mementos / mementoes
lick	lying	meow
lie	madam	messenger
life, lives	madness	metamorphosis
life cycle	magenta	metaphor
like	mahogany	matter
likeable	maid-of-honour	measles
lilac	mail	medically
lime	mammal	member
limited	mammoth	mercy
line	man, men	meridian
lineage	manageable	mermaid
lion, lions	management	mess
lioness	mangos / mangoes	message

meter	moral	nicely
metre	morning	nick
mice	mosquitoes	niece
microphone	moss	night
microscope	mother	nitrogen
midday	motion	no
midnight	mottos / mottoes	noise
mileage	mountain	normal
military	much	north
millennium	muck	not
milligram	multiple	notebook
millilitre	multiplication	notice
millimetre	mum	noticeable
million	mumbled	nought
mimicking	murky	noun
mineral	murmur	novel
miniature	murmuring	November
miniscule	muscle	nozzle
mint	mustard	nudge
minus	mutual	numerator
minute	nanny-goat	numerous
miracle	narrator	nursery
mirror	narrow	nutrition
misinterpret	national	oasis, oases
misrepresent	naughty	object
miss	navigate	observation
missile	navigation	observe
missionary	navy	obstacle
misunderstood	nearer	obstruct
misuse	necessary	obtuse
mixture	necessity	obvious
moaned	negative	occasion
mobile	neglect	occasionally
moccasin	neighbour	occupation
mock	neighbourhood	occupy
mode	neither	occur
model	nephew	occurred
molecule	nerve	occurrence
Monday	nervously	occurring
monkey, monkeys	nestling	ocean
monstrous	net	October
moo	never	octopus, octopuses
moose	news	off

offence	panel	percentage
offend	panic	perfect
offering	panicking	perilous
office	pants	perimeter
officer	paper	permission
offices	paraffin	perpendicular
official	parallel	perpetual
often	parallelogram	perpetual
omitted	parcel	persevere
omnivore	pardon	person
onslaught	pare	personal
ooze	parliament	petrified
opinion	parr	pharaoh
opportunity	parrot	pharmacy
oracle	part	phone
orange	particle	photo, photos
orchid	particularly	photosynthesis
ordinary	partner	physical
organ	party	physics
organise	pass	pianos
organism	passage	pick
origin	passed	picnicking
original	passer-by	piece
orphan	passive	pier
other	past	pierce
ought	patch	pig, pigs
ounce	pathetically	piglet
out	patios	pile
outrageous	patrol	pill
oval	pattern	pin
over	pause	pink
owl, owls	payment	pint
owlet	peace	pious
ox, oxen	peacock	pitch
oxygen	peahen	piteous
ozone	pear	place
pace	peck	plain
pack	peep	plane
pact	peer	planet
pair	pennant	planned
palette	pentagon	plant
pan	people	plateau, plateaux /
pancake	pepper	plateaus
		platypus

159

play	pretty	queen
please	previous	query
plenty	previously	questionnaire
pliers	price	queue
plod	priest	quick
plough	primary	quiet
plum	princess	quite
plunge	principal	quotation
polish	principle	quote
polite	prism	rabbit
politely	pro-government	raccoon
political	proceed	rack
pollution	process	radiance
population	product	radiant
pore	professional	radios
porridge	profile	radius
positive	profitable	raffle
possess	programme	rag
possession	project	rail
possibility	pronoun	rainbow
possible	pronounce	ram
post meridiem / p.m.	pronunciation	range
pot	propel	ratio
potatoes	propeller	rational
pounce	prophet	rattle
pound	protein	ray
powder	protested	reaction
power	psychic	read
practical	psychology	realistic
prance	punctual	really
precaution	punctually	reasonable
precede	puppy	rebel
precious	purple	recall
precipitation	purr	recede
predict	pursue	receipt
preferred	puzzle	receive
preferring	pyjamas	recently
prefix	pyramid	recognise
premature	quack	recollect
preoccupied	quarrel	recommend
present	quarry	record
press	quart	rectangle
pressure	quarter	recycle

red	revision	scaffold
reef, reefs	revolution	scale
reference	reward	scalene
referring	rhombus	scalpel
reflect	rhyme	scant
reflex	rhythm	scarce
refrigerate	rice	scared
refrigeration	riddle	scarf, scarfs / scarves
regard	ridge	scarlet
regatta	right	scatter
region	right angle	scene
regrettable	rite	scent
reign	rival	schedule
reindeer	river	scheme
relevance	roar	school
reliable	rock	science
relief	rocket	scissors
religion	roof, roofs	scoffed
rely	rose	scream
relying	rotting	scruffy
remain	rough	seagull
remark	round	seal
remember	row	search
repair	ruffle	season
replacement	ruler	seat
replacing	runner-up	second
replied	rural	secondary
reply	rustle	secret
replying	sack	see
report	sad	segment
represent	safety	seize
reproduce	sail	seldom
reptile	salmon	selfish
requirement	salt	selfishly
rescue	same	sell
resistance	sample	semicircle
resistible	sandwich	senseless
resources	sapphire	sensible
respiration	Saturday	sensitive
restaurant	saucer	sentence
reveal	sausage	separate
revere	savings	September
revise	saw	series

serious

servant

service

settle

severe

shallow

sharp

she'd / she would

she'll / she will

she's / she is

sheep

shelf, shelves

shield

shimmer

shirt

short

shouted

shower

shrieked

sick

sickly

sight

sign

signal

significance

significant

silhouette

silly

silver

simple

sincere

sincerely

singer

sir

sister

sister-in-law

site

sitting

sizzle

skeleton

skill

skip

skirt

skulk

slack

slavery

sleep

slick

slide

slipped

slither

slouch

slurp

smack

small

smile

smudge

snake, snakes

snarled

sneer

sneeze

sniff

sniggered

snooze

snorkel

soar

sobbed

soccer

sociable

social

society

soil

solos

something

son

song

sonnet

soon

sorrow

sorry

sort

sought

sound

source

south

sow

spaghetti

sparse

speaking

specialise

species

spectacle

speed

sphere

spinster

spiritual

splatter

spoonful

sport

spotty

square

squash

squeeze

squirm

stack

staff

stagger

stallion

star

statement

static

stationary

stationery

statue

status

steal

steel

stepfather

stepmother

stick

stiff

stomach

stoppable

stopped

storey

story

strapped

strategic

strawberry

stress

strive

student

studios

stuff

subdue

subject

substance

subtract

subtraction

succeed

success

successful

succumb

suck

suddenly

suffer

suffering

sufficient

summarise

summary

summer

summit

summon

Sunday

sunrise

sunset

super

superbly

supersede

supervise

supper

support

surgery

surplus

surrender

surround

survival

survive

swallow

swan

swim

swimming

syllable

syllabus, syllabuses / syllabi

symmetrical

synthetic

system

tabby-cat

tableau, tableaux / tableaus

tact

tadpole

tar

targeting

taught

taxing

teacher

tear

tease

technique

teenager

telephone

televise

television

temperate

temperature

temporary

tentacle

terrain

terrible

terrified

tertiary

textile

than

that

their

then

there

thermometer

thesis, theses

they'll / they will

they're / they are

they've / they have

thick

thief, thieves

thin

things

thirst

thorough

thought

threw

thrive

through

thud

thump

Thursday

tick

tier

tiger

tight

tile

timeline

tinkle

tiny

tissue

title

to

today

toffee

tom-cat

tomatoes

tomorrow

tongue

too

tooth, teeth

topical

tornado, tornadoes

torture

toss

tough

towards

towel

tower

town

trace

trade

traffic

trafficking	unnecessary	waffle
train	unreliable	wallow
translucent	unusual	walrus
transparent	urban	waltz
transportation	urgent	want
trapezium	use	war
tree	usually	ward
triangle	vaccinate	warm
trick	vaccination	warm-blooded
tricolour	vacuum	warrior
tricycle	valley	wasn't / was not
trolley	value	watch
trophy	van	water
tropics	vapour	water cycle
trot	veer	we'll / we will
trough	vehicle	we're / we are
trousers	vein	we've / we have
trudge	venue	weather
true	versatile	wedge
trumpet	vertebra, vertebrae	Wednesday
tub	vertebrate	weren't / were not
Tuesday	vertical	weigh
tundra	vessel	weight
tunnel	veterinary	weird
turkey, turkeys	victimise	wetness
turquoise	vile	whale
tweezers	village	wharf, wharfs / wharves
twice	villain	wheelchair
twilight	violet	when
two	virtual	where
tyranny	virus	which
umbrella	visible	whiff
unbelievable	visual	whip
uncle	visualise	whirl
understood	vitamin	whisper
unfortunately	vixen	whistle
unhappy	voice	white
unicorn	volatile	who
uniform	volcanoes	who's
unimportant	volume	whose
unison	volunteer	wick
unkind	voyages	wide
unless	waddle	wife, wives

wilderness
win
wind
window
windy
wireless
wish
withdraw
without
witness
wolf, wolves
woman, women
won't / will not
wonderful

woollen
worry
worthwhile
wouldn't / would not
wound
wrapping
wreck
wriggle
write
written
yacht
yard
year

yellow
yesterday
yield
you'd / you had
you'll / you will
you're / you are
you've / you have
youngster
your
zeros / zeroes
zoology
zoom
zoos

Your own Spelling list

First Aid in English Readers
Angus Maciver

Exciting stories from a wide variety of cultures!

These entertaining books include a wide variety of fiction, non-fiction and poetry from a range of genres.

They are beautifully illustrated to help engage students, and include comprehension questions and exercises to develop their writing skills.

First Aid in English Reader A – What a Fright 978 07169 50004
First Aid in English Reader B – Ali Baba 978 07169 50011
First Aid in English Reader C – Buried Treasure 978 07169 50028
First Aid in English Reader D – A Narrow Escape 978 07169 50035
First Aid in English Reader E – Crossing the Line 978 07169 55047
First Aid in English Reader F – Kariba 978 07169 55054

For more information on our full range of resources and to order, find your local agent by calling +44 20 7873 6240, or by visiting www.hoddereducation.com/agents.